Mitchell B. Cooper

Songs from the Heart

Book #1

With more to come

BALBOA
PRESS

A DIVISION OF HAY HOUSE

Balboa Press books may be ordered through booksellers or by contacting:

Balboa Press
A Division of Hay House
1663 Liberty Drive
Bloomington, IN 47403
www.balboapress.com
1 (877) 407-4847

Because of the dynamic nature of the Internet, any web addresses or links contained in this book may have changed since publication and may no longer be valid. The views expressed in this work are solely those of the author and do not necessarily reflect the views of the publisher, and the publisher hereby disclaims any responsibility for them.

The author of this book does not dispense medical advice or prescribe the use of any technique as a form of treatment for physical, emotional, or medical problems without the advice of a physician, either directly or indirectly. The intent of the author is only to offer information of a general nature to help you in your quest for emotional and spiritual well-being. In the event you use any of the information in this book for yourself, which is your constitutional right, the author and the publisher assume no responsibility for your actions.

Any people depicted in stock imagery provided by Getty Images are models,
and such images are being used for illustrative purposes only.
Certain stock imagery © Getty Images.

ISBN: 978-1-9822-0929-2 (sc)
ISBN: 978-1-9822-0930-8 (e)

Print information available on the last page.

Balboa Press rev. date: 09/04/2018

Contents

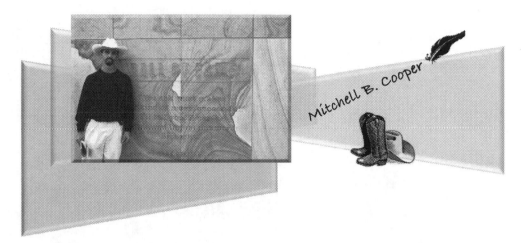

A Word from the Author: Mitchell B. Cooper

I began my journey in the world of poetry when I was only twelve. It was a way to express how I was feeling. My mom would come into my room to see what I had been writing to figure out what I was thinking about and how I was feeling. Love, pain, sadness, happiness, loneliness, all seem to end up in a poem. She started putting them in a notebook and that's when I got started saving my writings. And I love to get a request for a special occasion or maybe a special person to someone. My heart goes in to every word.

Since adulthood, I have turned to country singing. No, I don't sing, but the songs in my head that find their way to my tablets do sound pretty dang good. If only I could get just one recorded with a Country star, I would die a happy man. Yes, I am a dreamer and I thank God for my three awesome kids, my mom, my two brothers, my friends, the strangers who have inspired me and for every stroke of the pen. So here's to you.

I hope you read something familiar that speaks…

…From My Heart to Yours…

I dedicate this book as a legacy to my kids. MiKayla, Caleb, and Kaitlyn.
You 3 have been my strength and I hope you will always remember……
Your Dad is and will always be Your Dad and I Love You.

The Answer

You say you're looking for a miracle,
Someone who will steal your heart.
Not someone who will steal your love,
Then tear your world apart.
Well honey I've been here for years,
So why can't you see.
If you add up all you're looking for,
The answer will equal me.

You don't need to know algebra,
You don't even have to know Math.
'Cause it wouldn't take a rocket scientist,
To see what you could have.
That cabin will be our mansion,
Our fence will be those trees.
So you add up all you're looking for,
The answer will equal me.

Now I'm just a poor 'OLE country boy,
I don't have any money in the bank.
But I do have a roof over my head,
And a God upstairs to thank.
If you'd just stop for a moment and think,
You would know we're meant to be.
'Cause if you add up all you're looking for,
The answer will equal me.

You're always talking about other guys,
I just grind my teeth and grin.
Knowing good and well none of those fellows,
Will ever stand by you 'til the end.
Honey, please just open your heart,
Then I'm sure that you will see.
That if you add up all you're looking for,
The answer will equal me.

You don't need to know algebra,
You don't even have to know Math.
'Cause it wouldn't take a rocket scientist,
To see what you could have.
That cabin will be our mansion,
Our fence will be those trees.
So you add up all you're looking for,
The answer will equal me.

So go add up all you're looking for…The answer will equal me.

Your Best Friend Sam

He leaves his job around 10 PM,
Not even paying attention, to the homeless man.
Then walks to his brand new car again,
Well the man walks up with a knife,
The rich man screams, I've got two kids and a wife,
Here take my money.
Then he reached out his hand.
The homeless man looks and sheds a tear,
He says I can't believe you haven't seen me here,
I'm not a beggar Sir, I'm someone you know.
With those words he opened a note,
The rich man's eyes lit up when he spoke,
As he started the letter,
To my best friend Joe.
--And he read—

When we get home from this tour through hell.
I hope this letter finds you in good health.
Just believe in you country,
It won't let you down.
Because veterans are heroes,
Love you best friend… Sam!

When he heard those words tears started to flow,
He said I'm sorry friend I did not know.
And I have to say, I really didn't care.
The poor man says, well that's all right,
I have your letter to warm me on a cold night,
And it's worked so far, and it's been years.
The rich man says your coming home with me,
To be a part of my family,
Because I owe it to you, for saving my life.
When they pulled up his wife opened the door,
The look on her face said she hadn't seen him before,
Then the rich man said, "This is Sam."
And it lit up her eyes.
--And he said—

I wrote that when we got home, from our tour through hell.
I would hope that my letter found him in good health.
I believed in my country and it still let me down.
But veterans are heroes…
Yes veterans are heroes…
Love your best friend…Sam!!!

Jobs Like This

Dear Darling, I know we fought last night,
And I left, without saying goodbye.
But when I got to work,
And that bell rung again,
This time, it changed my life.

I saw a stranger, who had given his life.
Dead from smoke and burns, trying to save his wife.
Another hard fought battle,
Another time at risk.
And it's tough; yeah it's tough,
Jobs like this….

Last night I made a stop of a suspicious car.
About a mile down the road on 85.
They were fussing and swerving so I stopped them.
And this time it changed my life.

I saw a stranger, try to take my life.
By shooting at me three times, in front of his wife.
Another hard fought battle,
Another time at risk.
And it's tough; yeah it's tough,
Jobs like this…..

Whether you're a policeman, a fireman,
Or someone else saving lives.
It's time to stand up, and be recognized….

For one more hard fought battle,
One more time at risk.
And it's tough; yeah it's tough,
Jobs like this….

This Chair

He comes in, pulls up a stool, and orders an ice-cold beer.
He says I've had a bad day, so please don't say,
That I shouldn't be here.
I've been going crazy, ever since she walked out,
But I've sat and thought, of how to get her back,
And all my memories, lead me back to...
This chair.

Where I first saw her,
Like a moving blur.
I was too drunk,
To even say hello…
Back to this chair,
So many times I've been here.
But usually,
I could go back home.
But tonight it stops here…
Back at this chair…

Well it's half past nine, when he gets up to go.
Then pauses and takes one last look.
Says it's sure been fun, all the things we've done,
All the loving pictures we took.
So I'll see you around, some other time,
I'd say it probably wouldn't be here.
Unless all these thoughts I have,
Get me down and sad,
And lead me back to...
This chair.

Where I first saw her,
Like a moving blur.
I was too drunk,
To even say hello…
Back to this chair,
So many times I've been here.
But usually,
I could go back home.
But tonight it stops here…back at
This chair…

Yeah tonight it stops here.
Back at...This chair…

I'm Not Waiting

You came to work this morning, with tears in your eyes.
And told another story, trying to make it all right.
When I heard you, I just sighed,
And shook my head again.

You try to tell us, that he loves you so.
But love is something that he hasn't shown.
And I'm not waiting until you're gone,
To try and be a friend.

'Cause God made you,
To love and respect.
Not to be put down,
And not to neglect.
And I want stand and watch,
This again.
I'm not waiting until you're gone,
To be a friend.

A little trip at lunch, is all that it'll take.
To get this thing right, and get your life straight.
If you'll be strong enough, to walk away.
We can put him in the past.

So please don't stand there, and tell us more lies.
Or try to make up something, to make it all right.
'Cause I'm not waiting until that dreadful night,
To be a friend.

'Cause God made you,
To love and respect.
Not to be put down,
And not to neglect.
And I won't stand and watch,
This again.
'Cause I'm not waiting until you're gone,
To be a friend.

No I'm not waiting until you're gone,
To be a friend.

My Heart Stays Here

As the rain comes pouring down outside,
I sit here all alone.
With a thought in mind,
To put my past behind,
Get on my feet and get gone.

I loved you when you left me,
I probably always will.
But this home right here,
Is where I learned to care,
For the one that made my heart stand still.

My heart stays here,
With the love of my life,
I made a promise,
And I'll keep my word.
I said I would love her,
More than any other,
That's a promise,
I know she heard.
So my heart stays here…with her.

We had our good times together,
Lord knows we did.
By trusting each other,
By loving no other,
And by raising three beautiful kids.

I told you when you left me,
That my love for you is real.
And this home right here,
Is where I learned to care,
For the one who made my heart stand still.

My heart stays here,
With the love of my life,
I made a promise,
And I'll keep my word.
I said I would love her,
More than any other,
That's a promise,
I know she heard.
So my heart stays here…with her.
I made a promise…And I'll keep my word.

When You're In Love

When we met it was different, we both still believed in dreams.
Then as the years rolled by, we realized certain things.
Like the people we can trust, when we're down and out.
And the ones who believe in us, without any doubts.
Still we go at each other, then later we make up.
That's just how it is,
When you're in love…..

When you're in love,
You forget about certain things.
When you're in love,
You look forward to what tomorrow brings.
Whether it's Hell or it's Heaven,
Together you can live it up.
That's the way it is,
When you're in love….

Now here we stand together, after 20 short years.
Still laughing with each other, still drying each other's tears.
Happy that we made it, through so many rough times.
That just seems to follow, along our trails in life.
Still together we stand strong, and give thanks to our father above.
That's just how it is,
When you're in love……

When you're in love,
And the time comes to say goodbye.
When you're in love,
You know you'll meet again in another life.
Hell will just have to wait,
In Heaven we'll live it up.
That's the way it is,
When you're in love.

Yeah hell will have to wait,
In heaven we'll live it up.
That's how it's supposed to be,
When you're in love…..

Behind This Door

I heard the phone ring, in the hallway this morning,
I wondered who would call, at that time.
I listened so close, to what you told him,
Then I put my head on your pillow, and cried.

The words you spoke, sounded like music.
But the tune you played, I've never heard before.
So let me say this now, before you leave me girl,
You'll always have a home,
Behind this door.

Behind this door,
Where we laughed, fought, and cried.
Behind this door,
Where happiness once lived.
You'll always have a place.
If you're ever,
Behind this door again.

I'll help with your bags, while asking you to stay.
Still I know that your mind, has already been made.
So I won't beg and plea, no, my words have been said.
And behind this door, is where they'll stay.

Behind this door,
Where we laughed, fought, and cried.
Behind this door,
Where happiness once lived.
You'll always have a place.
If you're ever,
Behind this door again.

You'll always have a place.
If you're ever,
Behind this door again.

Still In My Life

I woke up early this morning,
And caught the end of the breaking news.
It seems a plane went down, on the outskirts of town,
They would have more before they were through.
I ran and got your flight number, and read it left at nine o'clock.
When I heard the time of the crash, was just a half past,
That's when my heart just stopped.

I screamed, "Honey, where are you now?
Did you miss your flight?
Someway or somehow.
And if you did,
Why haven't you called…
Then that call came in.
And my tears were dried again.
And replaced by pride.
That you were still in my life…..

It's been twenty years and counting, since that day in '79.
The doctors have all said, that I'm about dead,
It's just a matter of time.
Now it seems to be getting darker, but there's a light up ahead.
Then when that machine finally buzzed, I knew where I was,
Because I felt you take my hand.

And I screamed, "Honey, I've found you now.
You'll never leave again, no way or no how.
Because in my arms, is where you belong.
Then our call came in,
And my tears were dried again.
And replaced by pride.
That you were still in my life.

Yes I'm filled with pride,
That you are still in my life.

She's Heard It All

It's midnight, when he comes in.
Smelling like a brewery, once again.
Then he sits down on the couch, 'til four…

Well he thinks all night, about what to say.
When she starts asking, at daybreak.
But he know, she's heard it all before.

She's heard it all, from I got sick,
To I was shooting pool, down at Rick's.
From I got put in jail, and had nobody to call.
Yeah I'd about say,
She's heard it all…
Yeah she's heard it all.

Well it's five after six, and he pulls up.
With a cooler full of cokes, in his pickup truck.
And he doesn't seem to mind,
That the game ended at three.

Well he sits and thinks, about what to say.
But his girl has had it,
And she walks away.
Then she turned around and said,
This time it was me…

She's heard it all, when he lies to her mom.
Still she never thought,
That this day would come.
So with a strong voice,
She stood strong and tall.
And wiped her tears away,
And said I've heard it all.

So take her or take me,
And please just leave.
Because I've heard it all,
But this time it was me!!!

A Mother's Love

When we were young,
She taught us right from wrong.
Then when we failed,
Her fate stayed strong.
'Cause she knew,
How we were raised.
And she knew,
We'd make it big someday.

Then as we grew,
Into young men.
Her faith in us,
Was tested again and again.
But she never,
Let it show.
It's because of her,
That I know.

That a mother's Love,
Is a blessing to all.
The strongest man,
Could never climb those walls.
And nothing on earth,
Will ever be as strong,
As a mother's Love.

Now we're all grown,
And moved away.
To our own families,
In different states.
But we stay in touch,
Because we know.
The lessons we learned,
Many years ago.

About a mother's Love,
Being a blessing to all.
The strongest man,
Could never climb those walls.
And nothing on earth,
Will ever be as strong,
As a mother's Love.

No nothing on earth,
Will ever be as strong,
As a mother's Love

I Beg Your Pardon

Sitting alone in the bedroom,
Thinking about the words you said.
You know it broke my heart.
To think we would part,
Cause of something you thought I did.
I told you when we met I was different,
The words I love you so easily came.
Then on that first stormy night,
During our first thunderous fight,
You screamed that I was the same.

Well Honey I beg your pardon,
I don't believe what I just heard.
I've tried so hard to bring us together,
So please take back those words.
I'll admit my faults are plenty,
But with my mistakes I have learned.
So honey I beg your pardon.
I can't believe what I just heard.

I know there were times you were lonely,
I was always working overtime.
I refused to see,
That what I need.
Was the one thing already mine.
Then one night there came the answer,
The one I needed to open my eyes.
You said you needed a man,
That could understand,
So you guessed this was goodbye.

Well honey I beg your pardon,
I don't believe what I just heard.
I've tried so hard to bring us together,
So please take back those words.
I'll admit my faults are plenty,
But with my mistakes I have learned.
So honey I beg your pardon,
I can't believe what I just heard.
Honey I beg your pardon,
I can't believe what I just heard…

I Do Now

I overheard you this morning,
At our first break.
Say your wife finally walked out,
Last night about eight.
You were passing it off,
As being no big deal.
Then the fellas all walked out,
And the tears you shed were real.
--You said—

I never noticed,
How clean the house was.
And I never thanked you,
For that dinner so good…
I never realized,
How much you help me out.
But on thing's for certain,
I do now!!!

I couldn't sit there silent,
With you in so much pain.
So I walked up to you,
And said "Did you apologize…again!!!
Maybe she'll come back."
You said, "This time I think she's gone,
I just never noticed,
All the things she does at home…."
--Like—

I never noticed,
When the floors were gleaming bright.
And I never realized,
That my shirts didn't stay white.
I never realized,
How much you help me out.
But one things for certain,
I do now!!!

No I never noticed,
But I do now!!!!

Tonight I'm A Single Man

Tonight the world around me,
Crumbled and fell apart.
When she told me goodbye,
With the tears in her eyes,
Then went looking for a brand new start.
She said those familiar words,
She gave me the familiar line.
You've been great to me,
That I can see,
But I still need some time.

Tonight I'm a single man,
Free from hope and love.
Hanging out with friends,
Telling them same lies again,
About how I've had enough.
Tonight may soon be over,
So I'll flirt the best I can.
Hanging out with friends,
Telling them same lies again,
Because tonight I'm a single man.

I know I'll be sorry tomorrow,
But that won't stop me tonight.
Because somehow or someway,
When tonight becomes today,
I'll find a way to make it right.
So tonight I'll be at Lowry's,
Getting drunk and cheering on the band.
So don't let that sun rise,
To open up my eyes,
Because tonight I'm a single man.

Tonight I'm a single man,
Free from hope and love.
Hanging out with friends,
Telling them same lies again,
About how I've had enough.
Tonight may soon be over,
So I'll flirt the beat I can.
Hanging out with friends,
Telling them same lies again,
Because tonight I'm a single man.
I'll be hanging out with friends,
Telling them same lies again,
Because tonight I'm a single man.

Her Heart Walked Out On Me

She took the gold band off her finger,
She said her love for me had died.
She said I had broken her heart,
And that I tore her world apart.
So now her heart could never be mine.

She left my suitcase on the front porch steps,
With a letter that said goodbye.
My eyes slowly filled with tears,
As my mind wandered about the years,
When she was proud to be all mine.

Now I'm wondering what I have to do,
To finally make her see.
That I tried my very best,
To be better than all the rest,
Before her heart walked out on me.

I said that nothing worse could ever happen,
When my heart said you were gone.
You walked out the door crying,
You said you felt like you were dying,
But now you're wanting to run back home.

Now you know I feel so badly,
To say that we are through.
You say that I do not care,
And that I was never there,
To ever care for you.

Now I'm wondering what I have to do,
To finally make her see.
That I tried my very best,
To be better than all the rest,
Before her heart walked out on me
I tried my very best,
To be better than all the rest,
Before her heart walked out on me.

A Bumpy Ride

I'm opening up my heart to say I love you,
I'm reaching out a hand to help you see.
That anybody who ever said they love you,
Could never love you as much as me.
I'm knocking on a door that's never opened,
With hopes that my heart has the key.
That will take me into your arms at last,
And keep me there throughout eternity.

But whether that rock ever rolls is up to you,
You possess the strength I need to push it aside.
So please have faith in me and hang on to your seat,
Because this might just be a bumpy ride.

You told me once that you really loved me,
Then you turned right around and said drop dead.
You took all of my words and twisted them around,
Until they would no longer sound right in your head.
It's no wonder that your heart can't love me,
It's too busy holding on to broken dreams.
You say you've changed your mind but I'm still left behind,
Or at least that is how things seem.

So whether that rock ever rolls is up to you,
You possess the strength I need to push it aside.
So please have faith in me and hang on to your seat,
Because this might just be a bumpy ride.

Yeah have faith in me and hang on to your seat,
Because this might just be a bumpy ride.

Shooting Those Memories Down

Well how are you doing,
Where have you been.
Are you going home with me…?
Yes I'm sober.
That's what I told her,
Before I fell down to my knees…
I know she was gone,
Before I hit the floor.
Back out there painting the town…
So now I'm stuck here.
In this same 'OLE chair,
Shooting those memories down…

It might take, one, two, or three more beers.
You just can't ever tell…Until her memory,
Is gone from here, and I feel like myself…
So hey bartender, Keep them coming,
Right to this same 'OLE stool…I'll be here,
Shooting those memories down…
Just like a stubborn fool!!!

Yeah I'll be,
Shootin'em down all right,
So I want have time to talk…
So tell those ladies,
Asking for me,
The can all take a walk…
I'm going to be here,
All by myself.
I don't need nobody around…
Cause tonight I'm staying right here,
In my favorite chair,
Shooting those memories down…

It might take, one, two, or three more beers.
You just can't ever tell…Until her memory,
Is gone from here, and I feel like myself…
So hey bartender, Keep them coming,
Right to this same 'OLE stool…I'll be here,
Shooting those memories down…
Just like a stubborn fool!!!

I'll be shooting those memories down,
From this same 'OLE stool…

Ain't It Funny

Ain't it funny…When we were kids.
All those goofy things…That I did.
And how it never seemed
To catch your eye…

Ain't it funny…That as we grew.
I always seemed…To have a crush on you.
But you didn't even notice
That I was alive…

Ain't it funny…How time made it all go away.
Ain't it funny…It took till now for me to say.
That I love you…I need you,
And I'll always want you honey…
But now that we've grown…
With families of our own.
Looking back…Ain't it funny…
Ain't it funny!!!

Ain't it funny…When I was sick.
You would come over…To baby-sit.
And no matter what
You could always make me smile…

Ain't it funny…The way I got jealous.
When you went out…With those other fellas'.
But I figure you'd come back
After a while…

Ain't it funny…How time pulls you away.
Ain't it funny…That I never took time to say
That I love you…I need you,
And I'll always want you honey…
But now that we've grown
With families of our own
Looking back… Ain't it funny…
Ain't it funny!!!

Yeah looking back… Ain't it funny!!!

Nothing Is Free

I heard you on the phone,
Talking to your dad
Bragging about your life now,
And all the things you have…
You said it took time,
But now you acquire it with ease…
I think it's time that you learn,
Nothing in life is free…

Whether it's mowing the lawn,
Or washing your car,
Or picking up the trash,
The dogs have pulled in the yard…
You need to realize,
That you couldn't make it without me.
It's time that you learn,
Nothing in life is free…

No nothing is free…Nothing is giving.
It takes two people…To have the life you're living.
And you just don't realize…That it don't come with ease.
It might not take money…But nothing is free.

Now pretty soon they'll come,
To take me away…
So I want to say I love you,
More and more everyday…
I just with that you,
Could put yourself in my shoes…
And for once see the world,
Through my point of view…

You would see it's not always,
Going to come with ease…
It's time you learn,
Nothing in life is free…

No nothing is free…Nothing is giving.
It takes two people…To have the life you're living.
And you just don't realize…That it don't come with ease.
It might not take money…But nothing is free.

No it might not take money,
But nothing is free!!

Paper Plates And Plastic Forks

You say that you want better
Than what you have right here.
A single wide trailer,
Two tables and a chair.
You say this place ain't a home,
You're talking of divorce.
There's only two things to fight about,
That's paper plates and plastic forks.

Paper plates and plastic fords,
That's what it comes down to
Who will get our best possession?
It has to be me or you…
We lost our home the dog is gone,
So our lives are right on course.
All it comes down to,
Is paper plates and plastic forks…

I called my mom you called your dad,
We told'em we're moving home.
Said we'd had enough of each other,
We'd be better off on our own.
You told him the court dates set,
I'll drag him down in court.
'Cause there's no way I'll let him have,
Those paper plates and plastic forks.

Paper plates and plastic forks,
That's what it comes down to.
Who will get our best possession?
It has to be me or you.
We lost our home our dog is gone,
So our lives are right on course.
All it comes down to,
Is paper plates and plastic forks.

Yeah we lost our home the dog is gone,
So our lives are right on course.
All it comes down to,
Is paper plates and plastic forks…

It Would Be You...

Most of us live the hard life,
Most of us don't have it made.
We work all day and worry all night,
That the money will come our way.
Still I know that life is about,
I've traveled a dead road or two.
Still I know what life is about,
I've traveled a dead road or two.
But I'm not the type to sit and pout,
About the troubles we've been through.
If I could pick my future,
If I had just one more day.
I know I would be all right,
And I know just what I'd say.

It would be you when I wake each morning,
It would be you when I'm asleep at night.
It would be you that I'd be wanting,
Every minute that was left of life.
It would be you that I left crying,
Like I promised I'd never do.
But for it's worth if there's an angel on Earth,
Then honey it would be you...

I never dreamed I'd be so lucky,
To have an angel I could call my own.
They say most of us have one,
But too many never know.
I've been blessed for two years now,
With the one I call my better half.
She meets all of my expectations,
And beats any dream I've had.
Still if I could pick my future,
And have any dream come true.
I know I would be all right,
Because the dream would be you.

It would be you when I wake each morning,
It would be you when I'm asleep at night.
It would be you that I'd be wanting,
Every minute that was left of life.
It would be you that I left crying,
Like I promised I'd never do.
But for what it's worth, If there's an angel on Earth,
Then honey it would be you.
For what it's worth...If there's an angel on Earth,
Then honey it must be you!!!!

Right Here Tonight

As you lie in bed tonight,
I watch you lost in dreams.
I'm overwhelmed with pride,
That you are here with me.
You'll be gone with the rising sun.
Back again to his arms,
Regardless of what he's done.

So I sat up all night long,
To write down what I want to sat,
Just read this with an open mind,
Then I know you'll see it my way.

I did my best when you were little,
After your mother passed away.
But I had no idea,
How a girl should be raised.
I be damned if I will stand,
And let him take your life.
So this mess ends,
Right here tonight!!!

Ten years gone down the road,
My days are counting down.
I've made the call to yawl
'Cause I wanted my family around.
Your mama is waiting,
So dry those teary eyes.
This mess ends,
Right here tonight...

I did my best my whole life,
To raise you by myself.
But tonight your mama needs me,
To put this life down here to rest.
So be happy for me,
And please don't you cry.
This life was tough, I've had enough,
This mess ends right here tonight.

Yeah this life was tough,
I've had enough,
It ends right here tonight!!!!

Broken Hearted Cowboy

He comes home and cuddles up,
To the angel in his bed...
But it's the same story he's heard before,
She's got a pain, in her head...

So he sits all alone,
And he fights back the tears.
He know it's coming,
She's found someone,
And no longer needs him there.

He's a broken hearted cowboy,
He's never hurt like this before.
He's been stomped, kicked, bucked, and bit,
But this time it's his heart on the floor.
So he'll pull him up a bar stool,
And down him a few.
When you're a broken hearted cowboy,
That is what you do!!!

No more rodeo, no more saddles and spurs.
This time... he's home for good...
No more broken bones, no more late night calls
Saying he'd be there...if he could...

But she's heard it all before,
She has now turned a deaf ear...
He know it's coming,
She's found someone,
And no longer needs him there

He's a broken hearted cowboy,
He's never hurt like this before.
He's been stomped, kicked, bucked, and bit,
But this time it's his heart on the floor.
So he'll pull him up a barstool,
And down him a few.
When you're a broken hearted cowboy,
That's just what you do!

When you're a broken hearted cowboy,
That's just what you do!!!

Drunken Genius Sober Fool

He's running his mouth...once again,
While his buddy...is downing yet another.
He's bragging about...how smart he is,
While his friend...is lost in wonder.

Still through the eyes...of the woman,
That he has...been chasing.
She admires the way...the young man,
Admits the faults... that he's now facing.

He stutters I may be drunk,
But I know what I'm saying.
I drown my sorrows away,
While my buddy keeps playing.
I've accepted who I am,
Hell I think I'm pretty cool.
I would much rather be a drunken genius,
Than a sober fool!!!

For years now...it's been the same.
Every night...that they get together.
One heads...for the billiards.
While the bar...Calls to the other.

Still as the twilight beckons...and the band plays.
One is lining 'em up...while the other puts 'em away.
But from across the room...a smile crosses her face.
Even though he's drunk...she still admires his way.

He stutters I may be drunk,
But I'll never do you wrong.
I'll just drown my sorrows away,
Then I'll make my way back home.
I've accepted who I am,
I hope that's good enough for you.
I would much rather be a drunken genius,
Than a sober fool!!!

Yes I'd much rather be a drunken genius,
Than a sober fool!!!

After Five Years

It's been five years and counting,
And we're still going strong.
Still after five years,
There's things you don't know.
And even though you think you know it all,
After five years....you don't!!!

It's been five years,
Since the day I asked you out.
And after all we've been through,
You're still having doubts.
And even though you think you know it all,
After five years...you don't!!!

After five years,
You still have your fears.
And I can't believe,
How hard I've tried...
After five years,
You're still shedding tears,
And it's still me,
That wipes them dry...
So how could you doubt the way I feel,
After five years.

So stop what you're doing,
Think about it for a while.
After five years together,
You're still in denial.

After five years,
You still have you're fears,
And I can't believe,
How hard I've tried...
After five years,
You're still shedding tears.
But it's still me,
That wipes them dry...
So how can you doubt the way I feel,
After five years!!!

How can you doubt it still,
After five years!!!
After five years...

Two Honest Words

Why it is...you do certain things.
Like rolling round...under the covers,
With whatever stranger...the night brings.

I know I'm not around...late at night,
But honey...I have to work.
And now that we're here...eye to eye,
I want to hear...two honest words.

We're through...get lost,
Or whatever they may be.
I'm gone...your fault,
Yeah, blame it all one me.
But when the twilight finds you,
And the moonlight brushes your face.
You'll find that two honest words,
Is all it takes.

Another long night...out on the job.
I'm ready...to just hang it up.
But there's three reasons...that I've got,
Why I can't...on the dash of my truck.

You're right...you deserve much better,
Than a heart...always broke and hurt.
So now that we know...we won't see forever.
It'll only take...two honest words.

You're wrong...I'm right,
Whatever is easy for you.
I'm gone...tonight,
Mark my words we're through.
But when that break of dawn finds you,
And the sunlight brushes your face.
You'll find that two honest words,
Is all it takes.

Just two honest words,
That's all it takes.

That's Just Bull

Hello honey...how ya doing,
That's all it took...to set you off.
You started yelling...and boohooing,
'Cause you thought my heart...would turn soft.

Honey I've got you...and I've figured out,
Exactly why your eyes...are so brown.
It's all the bull...when you swear and promise,
That you still...want me around.

Well that's just bull...but that's just fine.
Go on breaking...this heart of mine.
Then one day you'll see...one day you'll find,
You'll no longer...own my heart and mind.
That's just bull!!!

Five years...we've been together,
Through Heaven...and through Hell.
Through the tears...we swore forever,
We would never again...be by ourselves.

Still honey I've got you...and I've figured out,
Why you're suddenly...so dark and tan.
It's all the bull...that you've been shoveling,
When you say...I'm your only man.

That's just bull...but that's just fine.
Go on breaking...this heart of mine.
Then one day you'll see...one day you'll find,
You'll no longer...own my heart and mind.
That's just bull!!!
That's just bull!!!

Northern Lightning, Southern Flames

You say you can feel the heat,
She's hotter than the flames of hell.
You said she walked right out your door,
And left you standing there by yourself.
You couldn't say a work,
She caught you off guard.
Now that northern Lightning and those Southern Flames,
Are burning up your heart...

Northern Lightning and Southern Flames
Today they're both burning bright.
Trying to outdo each other,
I tell you it's a darn good fight.
Still they go at each other,
Without laying the blames.
Now who'll catch the wind and finally win,
Northern Lightning or Southern Flames.

You say she took the bedroom,
And the kitchen was already hers.
She's advanced passed your guard line,
And left your defense in smoking embers.
She's building confidence, she's gaining ground,
She's burning up your heart.
With Northern Lightning and Southern Flames,
She has caught you off guard.

Northern Lightning and Southern Flames
Today they're both burning bright.
Trying to outdo each other,
I tell you it's a darn good fight.
Still they go at each other,
Without laying the blames.
Now who'll catch the wind and finally win,
Northern Lightning or Southern Flames.

Who'll catch the wind and finally win,
Northern Lightning or Southern Flame...

Keep Dixie Flying

Well they say I'm a racist,
But I've never hated anything.
So instead of judging my flag,
Try judging me...
You may see it as stars and bars,
But I see Southern Pride.
And I'll fight to the death, like the rest,
Just to see that she flies.
Now you Northerners might not like it,
But if I said I cared I would be lying.
The only thing I've got to say,
Is Dixie, keep it flying...

Yeah, keep OLE' Dixie flying,
Fly it high and proud.
If folks don't like it,
They can always leave the south.
So don't give up on Dixie,
If you do, it should be a crime.
So be proud of your southern heritage,
And keep OLE' Dixie flying...

Now I can already hear the critics,
Talking about what we must do.
Well, no politician speaks for me,
And they shouldn't speak for you...
Just stand up for your beliefs,
And those who died trying.
The flag is heritage, not hate,
So let's keep OLE' Dixie flying.

Yeah, keep OLE' Dixie flying,
Fly it high and proud.
If folks don't like it,
They can always leave the south.
So don't give up on Dixie,
If you do, it should be a crime.
So be proud of your southern heritage,
And keep OLE' Dixie flying...

Be proud to be...from the South,
Keep OLE' Dixie flying...

Guitars, Prison, And You

I thought about it last night,
Like I told you I would.
I still couldn't come up with anything,
That came close to sounding good.
You told me to get my life straight,
Then together we would see this through.
And I realized, what's driving me crazy,
Is guitars, prison, and you...

Guitars, prison, and you,
That's all I have on my mind.
I just play a tune, while I think of you,
And this prison just takes my time.
No matter how you say it,
That's what my life has come down too.
And when my time ends,
Three things I don't want to see again,
Is Guitars, Prison, and You...

Fifteen years and counting,
With only ten more to go.
Maybe even five,
If I get my parole.
You told me to get my life straight,
So here's what I'm gonna do.
I'm gonna forget bad memories,
Life guitars, prison, and you...

Guitars, prison, and you,
That's all I have on my mind.
I just play a tune, while I think of you,
And this prison just takes my time.
No matter how you say it,
That's what my life has come down too.
And when my time ends,
Three things I don't want to see again,
Is Guitars, Prison, and You...

Three things I know,
That I need to let go,
Is Guitars, Prison, and You...

When The Power Goes Out

It's half past nine,
When they pull in the drive.
With nothing but a good time,
On their mind.
They'll have some drinks,
They'll scream and shout,
And they won't slow down
When the power goes out.

'Cause one of them boys,
Will bring some ice cold beer.
We'll have a campfire burning,
Over there.
We'll cook a pig in the ground,
And turn the music up loud.
Then party all night,
When the power goes out...

We'll put some candles in the hall,
To light the way.
To our only bathroom,
For emergency sake.
Then we'll eat and drink,
Just to pass the night.
'Cause it'll be a long time,
Before the morning light.
But 'til that sun rises,
We're gonna scream and shout.
That's what country folks do,
When the power goes out...

'Cause one of them boys,
Will bring a fishing pole.
And we'll go out,
By the watering hole.
Put a wager on,
Who'll catch the biggest fish.
When the power goes out,
We just party like this...

Yeah, We'll eat and drink,
Scream and shout...
Then party all night,
When the power goes out...

I'm Gonna Get It Right

If God could've created a prettier woman,
He must have not figured it out.
'Cause I've never met a prettier woman,
Than the angel that I've got now.
Sure, you fuss and holler,
But the way you work, you have that right.
So I try my best every chance I get,
To pull you close and hold you tight.
--Then I whisper--

The kids are gone...We're all alone...
So what do you want to do?
A meal prepared just right...
Out by a candle light.
Is just the beginning…
Of what's waiting for you.
I just want you to see...
What you mean to me.
I hope this will open your eyes…
'Cause I try my best.
Every chance I get…
And tonight...
I'm gonna get it right.

We've had some pretty tough years,
But we have made it through.
And I've never said how proud,
That I am I am of you.
But I'm gonna make it up to you,
Starting tonight.
While I'm pulling you close,
Beneath the twilight....I'll whisper.

I did what you said...And made up the bed...
So tell me what you want to do.
A nice hot bath...Then I'll rub your back...
Or we can sit and I'll talk to you.
I want you to know...That I love you so...
So it's long stemmed roses tonight.
'Cause even though I try my best...Every chance I get...
Tonight...I'm gonna get it right.

Yeah I try my best...Every chance I get...
But tonight...I'm gonna get it right.

Tired Of The Pain

Doctor, Doctor...Help me out,
I don't know what's going on.
I found a letter...That said she was tired of the pain,
On the table when I got home.
So I rushed right over,
But they won't tell me anything.
Can I see her...is she awake,
There's so many things to say."

"Like I didn't know she was hurting.
I didn't see any signs.
The only problems I've seen,
Were those silly problems of mine.
And I swear I'll pay more attention,
If you can make her OK.
She said she was tired of the pain,
So please make it go away."

Well the doctor starred back at me,
And said, "Son, what are you talking about.
I haven't had any patient come in.
All of mine have been walking out."
I said, "But there ain't no other doctor,
And she wrote that she was tired of the pain.
So she had to come here hurting.
Please, would you check again?"

He said, "Son, she's not here,
But I believe I know where she is."
He said, "She comes through here all the time,
All of us are her friends.
She's down the block at the bar,
Drinking her problems away.
She said she shoulders all your problems,
And son she's tired of the pain."

Yeah, please make it go away....
She's tired of the pain.

To Make Ends Meet

When I was young, I was raised,
To never turn my back, or except the praise.
And as I grew, with my own kids,
I still preach the lessons...That my grandpa did.

He used to say, "Son, if you want to make it in life...
You need a steady job...and a loving wife...
You need breakfast in the morning...And church three times a week...
That's all you need in this world...To make ends meet..."

Now the years have passed...and grandpa passed on.
To a better life...than he's ever known.
And I talk to him nightly...letting him know that he's missed.
And every night before I go to sleep...I leave him like this.

I say, "Grandpa...I've had a good life...
By following your footsteps...by living right...
I eat my breakfast in the morning...
And I'm thankful for what's been given me...
I may not have a lot...But I make ends meet..."

I'm thankful that grandpa...watches over me...
It may not seem like a lot...
But it makes ends meet...

Leave My Flag Alone

First it was for heritage,
Now they're crying foul.
And they want to bring down my flag,
They say it doesn't speak for the south.

Well excuse me there Mister,
You need to search the History of the flag.
'Cause a lot of folks died to see her fly,
And there's nothing racist about that.

I've got a message for you Mister,
Think about it hard and long.
Don't start trouble where it doesn't exist,
Leave my Flag alone.....

So you want to say it's racist,
Well whites and blacks both fought the war.
And those who are starting trouble,
Don't even know what that was for....

You celebrate your heritage,
For a whole month respect is shown.
So try respecting my heritage too,
And leave my Flag alone.

Now don't go causing trouble,
By calling a boycott over our flag.
'Cause a lot of folks died to see here fly,
And there's nothing racist about that.

So take this message Mister,
Think about it hard and long.
Don't start trouble where it doesn't exist,
Leave my Flag alone.

So those who say it's racists,
Well you're just plain wrong.
So just leave my Flag alone!!!!!

Hard Working-Woman

The kids get home...about 3 o'clock.
That still doesn't mean...that her day has stopped.
She's got a full-time job...while they're at school.
Then she cleans and cooks...when her first job's through.
That's how it goes...for those hard-working women today.

They go to T-ball practice...have to be there by five.
And she can't forget...to bring the drinks tonight.
Then there's a grocery store...
Where they can stop on their way home.
For those hard-working women...
That's just how it goes.

That's how it goes...every day in life.
They're mother and healer...
And shopper and wife.
They don't receive...the credit they are due.
So to those hard-working women...
This one's for you!!!

Now it's supper time...she comes rushing in.
And words couldn't describe...that angel's grin.
When she looked in the kitchen...
At a table already set.
For my hard-working woman...
This is what you get.

A dinner for two...out by a candle light
Where we can enjoy each other...
In peace and quiet.
Tonight I'm gonna show...
The love I feel for you.
For my hard-working woman...
This one's for you!!!

Don't Say Goodbye

We packed up again today
And raced down that road.
To a doctor who was waiting,
To deliver that fragile load.
Then a smile came,
And you slowly closed your eyes...

I was stroking your hair,
Like I always do.
'Til the doctor burst in,
Between me and you.
Then I sat down,
And slowly I cried,
Don't say goodbye...

Don't say goodbye,
After just five years.
I've waited for my angel,
Finally you're here.
And I don't want,
To lose you tonight.
So please say you'll stay,
Don't say goodbye...

Now here we are,
50 years have passed.
You say that they're here,
To take you home at last.
Then I gave you a kiss,
And you slowly closed your eyes.
Then I sat down,
And slowly I cried.

Don't say goodbye...
It shouldn't be this way.
I finally got an angel,
For the angels to take.
And I don't want,
To lose you tonight.
So please say you'll stay,
Don't say goodbye...

Say you'll stay...Don't say goodbye.....

Junkpile Of Hearts

She woke in a fiery,
Said she thought about what I said...
She had thought it through,
About what to do,
Now she wished I was dead.

She packed her bag, walked out the door,
Looking for a brand new start.
So now I'm sitting here,
In my favorite chair,
Amidst a junk pile of hearts.

A junk pile of hearts...
That's what she's left behind...
Her new addition...
To her heartbreak mansion...
Just had to be mine...
So tonight I'm feeling lonely...
I'm taking it to hard...
She just walked away...
And let my dying pride lay...
In a junk pile of hearts...

She left me here...to dry up my tears,
Tonight I'm gonna start.
To forget the past...and at last,
Climb out of this junk pile of hearts.

A junk pile of hearts...
That's what she's left behind...
Her new addition...
To her heartbreak mansion...
Just had to be mine...
So tonight I'm feeling happy...
I'm no longer taking it hard...
I'm glad she walked away...
And let me stay...
In this junk pile of hearts...

She just walked away...
And let my dying pride lay...
In this junk pile of hearts...

The Hero

Times running out, the clock is ticking,
And the game is on the line.
He looks in the stands, at all the fans,
And the thought crosses his mind.
If he hits this shot,
He'll be the hero today...

Across town, at the same time,
She's teaching her son to swim.
She don't let him know, but she stays so close,
So danger stays away from him.
If he makes this lap,
He'll be the hero today...

Well, we all have dreams...
And we all have plans...
That's the way life goes...
But it's the time they take...
To watch them swim or play...
That makes them heroes...
So if you do nothing else...
Be the hero today.

It may not be much, in this world,
But someday it will come back.
So give them this day, watch them play,
You couldn't give any better than that.
And in their eyes,
You'll be the hero of the day.

We all have dreams...
And we all have plans...
That's the way life goes...
But it's the time you take...
To watch them swim or play...
That makes you a hero...
So have fun and play...
And be the hero today.

No matter what,
Be the hero today.

The American Public

You see them all over, every single day...
Wishing for a better life.
Still they push on, through the pain...
Just trying to get by.

They're digging ditches, they're planting trees,
Making this world a better place.
They're building bridges, they're raking leaves,
For the few dollars they are paid.

They are the American Public...
Made up of all different types.
Working hard together...
Regardless of black or white.
Isn't it sad when the bell sounds...
To some the friendship ends.
We're all the American Public...
Isn't it time we were all friends.

You come home at night; cut the TV on,
And it never seems to fail.
There's some racist views; on the news,
Casting all others to Hell.

But in this country, we just listen,
'Cause even ignorance has a right.
And if we can just stand strong; then before long,
We would all be friends in Life.

The American Public...
Is made up of all kinds...
Working hard together...
Regardless of black or white.
Isn't it sad that when that bell sounds...
To some the friendship ends.
We're all the American Public...
Isn't it time that we were all friends.

Yeah we're all the American Public...
Isn't it time we were all friends.

A Cool Breeze Blows

A cool breeze blows,
Inside I know;
Winters not far away....
By a fire at home,
Is where I belong;
But will it be that way...

The birds sing a song,
I hum along;
Nothing to do now no ways...
The time goes fast,
As another day goes past;
Out in these old sun rays.

Tammy and I,
Just sharing time;
I love it
And I hope she knows...
I still desire,
Nights by the fire;
As a cool breeze blows......

Mowing Old Memories Down

She came in...like a hurricane's wind,
And started throwing things...around the house.
She found out...I'd been running round,
Said it took some time...to find out.

She said she had a plan...to get even,
Then I heard...that back door slam.
Now she's fighting back tears,
While she's shifting gears,
And moving old memories down.

Well first she took the rosebush,
That I bought when we first met.
Then around the corner, to the other,
But it was too hard to get.
I told her to come inside,
And let's try to talk it out.
But she's made up her mind,
To leave the past behind,
And start mowing old memories down.

She burned up...all my clothes,
And threw my trophies...out on the lawn.
I yelled...watch what you're doing.
She said don't worry...they won't be there long.

Then as I was sitting down...I figured,
That all this...would blow over
Then I heard a buzz...I knew what it was.
That woman...had started the lawnmower.

Well she took the ashes from the clothes...
And my trophies were gone in a flash...
Then she slowed down...and turned around...
Then started coming back...
I told her I was calling the police...
I told them to get right over...
I said she's hopping mad...
She's coming back,
To mow me down on my lawnmower.
She's just mowing old memories down...

The Booze Blues

He arrives home from work,
With nobody to come home too.
So he dusts off his cowboy hat,
And polishes up his boots.
He grabs his spare change,
Then out the door he goes,
To drown old memories down,
At the bar down the road.

Well he's three sheets to the wind,
When the band starts to play.
He would love to go out dancing,
But right now he can't.
So he sits there at the bar,
And ponders his next move.
But tonight he'll just drown away,
He's got the booze blues...

Tomorrow, the sun will rise,
And he'll head off to work.
With a head that keeps pounding,
And a heart full of hurt.
Then when that five o'clock rolls around,
He'll stay true to his routine.
He'll head back down to the bar,
To his favorite chair, to drink.

Well he's getting rowdy,
When the band starts to play.
He asks her to dance,
But she kindly says no thanks.
So he sits down at the bar,
And ponders his next move.
But tonight he'll only drown away,
Those lonely booze blues....

Yeah tonight he'll just drown away,
Those lonely booze blues.

Watching Here Kinlling Me

I overheard her last night, talking to her mom on the phone.
She told her nothing was right, everything was going wrong.
Then I caught my reflection, and it made me think.
I was just standing by, watching her killing me.

I've never had…more forehead than hair.
And now instead of black…there's only gray up there.
And I've never noticed…those wrinkles around my eyes.
Just looking at me now…makes me won't to cry.

But instead I stand here staring…at a hope that I can't see.
Just looking in the mirror…watching her killing me.
Now I promised when we met, that I would always be here.
And that my love and time, would always be hers to share.

I've kept my word, while she's slipped on by.
Making plans without me, nearly every night.
And someday soon I pray, that she'll wake up and see.
That I can't always stand by, and watch her killing me.

I've never had my nerves…shake my hands in anger.
And now instead of love…there's only hope and pain here.
And lately I've noticed…how she loves to ride around.
Just thinking of where she's been…has given me a constant frown.

But instead of leaving I take it…I pray that she can see,
That the way her heart loves…Is killing me.
Someday soon I hope…That she'll wake up and see.
That watching her love…Is killing me.

Wilderness Mans' Dream

The business man says,
This is a waste of land.
But it's a paradise,
To the wilderness man.
With a campfire burning,
Out by the creek,
And a big black bear,
Staring back at me.

That's what they call,
The wilderness mans' dream....

My wife, her dad,
And some friends of ours,
Go out camping,
In the land of the bears.
With some rainbow trout,
Prepared to eat,
And those bright shining stars,
Up above me.

That's what they call,
The wilderness mans' dream....

The wilderness mans' dream...
That's what it is...
Load up the coolers....
And round up the kids...
We're going camping....
Out in the woods...
Where the bears and the fish...
Are the neighborhood...?
That's what we do...
On days like these...
We're just out here living
The wilderness mans' dreams...

Yeah we're out here living...
The wilderness mans' dreams....

Champions In God's Eyes

He sits in his wheelchair....all afternoon,
Just hoping...for some change.
He used to be a track star....man he flew,
Until a drunk...took that away.

He may not be able to walk now,
But he gladly moves on with life.
And no matter what he does in this world,
He's a champion in GOD'S   eyes.

She comes in from the night shift...changes clothes,
Then rushes...out the door.
She's got a part time job...in the morning,
And a child...to pick up at four.

She may not have it easy,
But still she pushes on with life.
And whether or not she makes it,
She's already a champion in GOD'S eyes.

Champions in GOD'S eyes...
That's exactly what they are...
They've been struggling for so long...
Through times that's been real hard...

Still they find the courage...
While others just give up on life...
They set the example for us to follow...
They are champions in GOD'S eyes...

So the next time you hear,
A tin cup rattle,
Or see the woman so tired,
She just can't walk.
Think of some words of wisdom,
Give a compliment...when you talk.

Cause they're the ones with all the courage...
You don't see them giving up on life...
And they may not be much in this modern world...
But they are champions in GOD'S eyes...
They may not succeed in this world...
But they are champions in GOD'S eyes...

An Angel In You

When we started out…
We could last through anything…
And there was seldom a time…
We were apart…

You were an angel…
You were my Queen…
And the only love…
Deep inside my heart…

You swept me up…
The day I met you…
And for once I was proud…
In the man that I loved…

You were my savior…
You were my king…
And I knew you had come…
From above…

From the heavens…
There came a message…
So clear this time…
That I knew…

That she'd never give up on me…
That he'd be here for eternity…
I could tell the message was true…
I had found an angel in you…

Patience Pays Off

I've seen em' on the corners, just giving up on life.
'Cause something or somebody, didn't treat them right.
So today I stopped and asked, the one circling ads in the classifieds.
"Sir would you like a helping hand?"
He just looked at me and smiled……

He said,
"I had faith in my father….but he left when I was seven.
To join my mother up above…. in the golden streets of Heaven.
I promised him that I would try."
He said in a voice so caring and soft…
"Have patience with the Lord….son,
'Cause patience pays off!!!"

Well, I got to the bar, and asked what he wanted to eat.
He said sir…I don't have no money, I said friend it's all on me.
Then while he was finishing up, I took out a business card.
I asked how would you like a job,
By the way I own this bar………

The homeless man sat silent, as the tears started to fall.
He said I told my daddy I'd have faith, but I've really had none at all.
He said, "I appreciate the offer"…I interrupted, "You can start anytime at all".
I'll have faith in you, if you just stay true."
He cried, "Daddy, patience does pay off!!!!"

He said, "I had faith in you daddy….though when you left me was only seven….
I've prayed every night to mother's light….glaring off the streets of Heaven….
I promised I would always try….
And that promise has not been lost.
I've always had patience with the Lord….
And patience does pay off….."

Yes, I've had patience with the Lord…
And patience pays off!!!"

Why On Earth

You know nobody like him... or the way that he lives.
All he does is take away....from you and the kids.
I agree with your mama.......for the first time in my life.
She told you she didn't like him...
So why on Earth would I???

Why on Earth would I standby.....
And not say anything......
Why on Earth should I be nice....
When he treats you so mean.......
You say it's none of my business......
If you choose to get hurt by him.....
I took your side the first time.....
Why on Earth would I do it again....

Well, it's half past nine in the morning...he comes pulling up the drive.
When he saw that Remington on the front porch...he thought he'd better just ride by.
You said to mind my business...my business is staring me in the eye.
You didn't think mama would stand for this....
So why on Earth would I???

Why on Earth would I standby...
And not say anything....
Why on EARTH should I turn my head....
And ignore what I've seen....
You say it's none of my business....
If you have a fight with him......
But I've let it slide one to many times....
Why on Earth would I do it again....

Yeah, I let it slide......
To many times....
Why on Earth would I do it again.....

Package Included

Excuse me mam'….I didn't mean…
To hog all the chairs…
I'd be glad to have you…sit near me…
Oh, the stories we could share…..

Yes, I'm sure…you've heard that before…
After all, you seem so charming….
Don't walk away…you can rest assure…
I mean your heart no harm….

It's just I'm a man…Like few other men….
I have to put my children….Before me and what I plan on doing….
Yes, I understand….But, I will not bend….
And I'll offer…no excuses…
I'm a man that comes….Package included!!!!

Yes, she looks like her mom…and that boys just like me…
I would love to hold you…
But I've got plans…
Today my baby is turning three….

So, here's my name…here's my number…
I really hope to hear from you…
Just keep in mind…if you take me under…
There's a package you must include!!!

'Cause, they're not leaving….And I'm not either….
They come before…..What I plan on doing!!!!
Keep that in mind….while you're alone this evening…
And I'm at home…thinking about you…
I'm a man that comes…Package included….

Yeah, like it or not….
There's a package included!!!!

A Man With Pride

12:45 I heard the shot, I knew I was too late.
He took his life like he said, he didn't want to die in pain.
I slowly got up from my bed, and wiped away some tears.
Then called up the local sheriff, and said......
You need to get over here.......

'Cause a man just died......
With his pride....
He went out with one shot....
Said he wouldn't hope...
For anyone to grow old....
With the disease that he's got.
Said he should be remembered...
For what he did here...
Not for needing someone at his side.
So don't shed a tear...
For what happened here...
'Case a man just died with pride.

Days rolled on "till it was time, I told my wife to kiss the kids.
Said I'll be watching over yawl from above,
I don't want them to see me like this.
So close the door load up the car, don't let a tear fall from your eyes.
'Cause I'm going like daddy did
A man with pride...

I'll be a man with pride....
When I die...
I'm going out with an inner peace.
I wouldn't hope...
For anyone to grow old...
Suffering through this disease.
I want to be remembered....
For what I did here...
Not for needing someone by my side.
So don't shed a tear...
For this man right here...
'Cause this man will die with pride.

Don't shed a tear...
For what happened here...
'Cause a man just died with pride.....

-End-

Hillbilly Heaven

It's 5:00 AM…the alarm goes off.
He's out the door… to feed the hogs
Then it's breakfast time…when the sun come up.
The cows are out again…so bring your truck!
That's the way it goes…In Hillbilly Heaven

He works all day…cut and baling hay,
Then hauls it to the barn…at the end of the day.
She's waiting in the door…when he gets back home…
Her smiling faces…says there is nothing wrong
That's the way it goes…Down In Hillbilly Heaven…….

Hillbilly Heaven…Where your neighbor's your friend….
It's an eyesore…to the business man…
But he's satisfied with the life he's been given.
That's the way things work…Down in Hillbilly Heaven…
Yeah it's Hillbilly Heaven…

When his time comes…He'll say "Don't fuss or fight.
I'll be fine where I'm going…I've lived life right.
All of my life, I've love and I've given…
That's how I know it….I'll go to Hillbilly Heaven….
Hillbilly Heaven…

Hillbilly Heaven…Where the water runs clean…
And the hilltops are full…with trees that are green…
That cabin in the sky…is where I'm heading…
That's the way things work…Up here in Hillbilly Heaven….
It's Hillbilly Heaven…

I'm satisfied with the life I was given…
I'm glad to be home in Hillbilly Heaven…

-End-

Happy Father's Day To The 3 Of You

Growing up I wasn't jealous,
Of my friends who had "dads".
But as good as they had it,
They didn't have what I had.
See I am not resentful,
I don't regret the life dealt to me.
Cause while all of my friends had a dad,
Well guess what, I had three!!!!
I had 2 older brothers…
That I still idolize.
They sometimes took me with them.
And let me hang out with "the guys"
They took me to the beaches…..
Far away from our little home.
Places I would have otherwise...
Never been or known.
They taught me how to drive…
And how to swing a bat,
Even taught me to shoot hoops.
And how to wear my hat.
They showed up at all my games,
And were the rowdy section of the crowd.
Even when I wasn't playing,
They were always cheering pretty loud.
On the other hand there is my mother,
Who had to double as a dad?
Looking back now that I have 3 young ones,
I don't see how we had all we had.
I recall her working 2 jobs,
At the cleaners, golden pantry and more..
Just to see we had what we needed,
Even if it wasn't bought from a store.
So don't weep for me this father's day,
I will be celebrating and giving love to all.
Cause as I remember growing up,
I had a father in you all.
I hope your day is glorious,
And I hope you spend it with your family.
I just wanted to say "happy father's day",
It just so happens that I had three......
Love you all....hope you have a great father's day

Written by: The smallest one, Mitchell B. Cooper
Dedicated To: My mother and my 2 brothers (Liz, Michael, & Marcus)

Dear God, Do You Have Some Time

Dear god do you have some time,
perhaps you could lend an ear.
I'm lost in this thing called life,
I find only trouble here.
I've thought about the reasons,
I'm positive that I'm to blame.
So I try not to hold grudges,
I'm not saying no names.
I thank you every morning,
for the day I get to see.
I bow my head every night,
to pray for help for me.
I'm lost without direction,
no GPS can help my travels.
But I would like a little mercy,
so my nerves don't stay rattled.
I have so much to be thankful for,
that granddaughter tops the list.
But I also have many more,
like my own 3 awesome kids.
I'm thankful for my 2 outstanding brothers,
who have always been at my side.
I'm thankful for my mother,
and even my past bride.
I'm thankful for the friends I've made,
and the adventures we've been on.
I'm thankful for the shelter I have,
in this cozy home.
I'm thankful Lord and you know it,
you can see what's in my heart.
You see more than this worn out path,
that's torn me all apart.
I'm thankful for my love of music,
and of poetry too.
I must admit to everyone,
I got that poets heart from you.
I'm thankful for the time I have left,
and I hope I serve you well.
I'm thankful that my soul is saved,
and won't know those flames of hell.
I'm thankful Lord for the beautiful day,
and the memories I get to keep.
I'm thankful to you for your time,
now please watch over me as I sleep.....
Amen...

I Need You Here Today

It seems as though you've been gone for years, my heart aches so much.
I still want to hear your voice, and I long for your touch.
I know someday we'll be together, but I don't know if I can wait.
I need your strength, and your love here today......

We shared so many memories, the walls show me the times.
When I could look into those eyes of yours, knowing everything would be fine.
I look at all the precious moments, we shared in every way.
I need your strength, and your love here today....

(Chorus)
Today when I wake up,
I will need you by my side.
Today when I rise up,
I will need you for the ride.
Today is gonna be painful,
And make it....I just may.
But one thing is for certain,
I need you today....

The grass is getting taller, I've not worried about that before.
There are trees that need to be trimmed, before those spring time storms.
Yeah I've come to realize, I miss you in so many ways.
One thing is so clear, I need you here today.....
*
Today when I wake up,
I will need you by my side.
Today when I rise up,
I will need you for the ride.
Today is gonna be painful,
and make it....I just may.
but one thing is for certain,
I need you today....

yeah one thing is for certain,
I still need you here today....

written by: Mitchell b. cooper
dedicated to: a good friend.... hope you like it

Snow, Snow, Go Away

Snow, snow,
Go away...
I'm getting too old,
To get out and play.

No sled to slide,
No snowman to make.
So take it away,
Send not another flake.

Let the power stay on,
Let the house stay warm.
Let the kids come together,
Like a beehive swarm.

Let those that travel,
Make their destination.
Let me go on,
A tropical vacation.

Let us enjoy the beauty,
Of the snow covered trees.
Let the trees stand strong,
In this deep freeze.

It sure is pretty,
But all I have to say.
Is snow, snow,
Please go away.......

Hello I'm Cupid

Hello it's me cupid,
the one you're waiting on.
I will see you tomorrow,
then I will be gone.

I got my arrows sharpened,
put new string on my bow.
Now I'm looking for some lovers,
who are clueless and don't know.

Maybe a reminder to buy her flowers,
to start out my day.
Maybe a box of mixed chocolates
will melt her heart away.

Maybe a little love song

will help the lady rest.
But if you're smart son its diamonds,
that a woman loves the best.

So I will do my part,
I'll strike her with the loving touch.
The rest is in your hands;
after all she prefers your touch.

So be brave and take a chance,
I promise she won't think you're stupid.
And son I know what I'm talking about,
after all, I am cupid.......

Happy early Valentine's Day everyone…

He Said Trust Me..... She Said Sure

The tear fell down, to the ground;
Her heart was broke into....
She sat and cried, for the man who died;
Whom she'd always held onto...
Through the tears, she shed her fears;
And asked god to take the lead.....
God told her to stand, and take his hand;
That's all she'll ever need....

It worked real well, as far as I could tell;
She was happy now it seemed....
She put the past behind, out of mind;
And reached for better things...
Through her travels, she came unraveled;
A time or two I know....
But she was holding the hand, of the man;
Who could make it all just go....

And he said trust me...She said sure.
He said my child I will love you...forevermore...
Just call on me...like you never have before.
He said trust me...she said sure...

Years went by, things were right;
Her new family was doing fine...
She still saved a part, of her heart;
To remember what she left behind...
Every night by her bed, she bows her head;
And pours out her soul...
To the man, still holding her hand;
Who could make it all just go.....

And he said trust me...She said sure.
He said my child I will love you...forevermore...
Just call on me...like you never have before.
He said trust me...she said sure...

Just call on me...Like never before.
Do you trust me...She said sure......
My child just trust me,
She said sure....

Folders On A Shelf

Some things I just remember,
I don't know why….I just do.
Then important things get lost,
As time pushes them out of view.
Still I have my own keepsakes,
I keep all to myself.
There in a box… in the closet,
In the folders on a shelf….

There are pictures of our daughter,
And the things she gave to me.
Like instructions to cooking chicken,
10 minutes at 9 degrees.
There are things she made at school,
I still treasure and I love.
They're all right there…wrapped with care,
In her folders on shelf one….

I remember how scared I was,
Just 2 years down the road.
When all of a sudden,
That boy came along.
Lord how he did change me,
But in case I do forget.
There's a reminder in my closet,
In the folders on a shelf.

There are pictures of his birthday…
In his high chair covered in cake.
There're drawings and hot wheels…
And his Dale, Jr. #8.
There's that armband from the ER…
When he wasn't in a healthy mood.
They're all right there…wrapped up with care…
In his folders on shelf #2.

Last of all…but not least…
That terror we gave life.
Looks just like her daddy…
Acts like her Mother alright.
There're pictures, awards, and a tape……
So that I could hear her sing.
In a box in the closet…
In her folder on shelf #3…

Yeah all my memories are in the closet….
In a box….In folders…to ME!!!

Just In A Different Place

Church was great like always,
Just in a different place.
I didn't find it odd because,
God is found any place.

I listened and I was focused,
I enjoyed my time there.
With people as close as family,
All heads bowed in prayer.

I know Mrs. Cricket missed me,
But she's with me in my heart.
The devil can't stop that,
Or tear my faith apart.

So God I say thanks again,
For your mercy and grace.
Church was great like always,
Just in a different place.....

Georgia Clay

Another hot day baking,
Out on this Georgia clay.
Time to sit and write a few,
Just passing the day away.
I'd like to be out on the lake,
Or on the beach somewhere.
Just writing with a chilled glass,
On the arm of my chair.

It's another hot day baking,
And summer has just begun.
Time for some sand and sea,
And a little southern fun.
I'd like to be casting sail,
And headed out to sea.
Or laying around in the shade,
Of a giant coconut tree.

It's another hot day baking,
So I believe that I will go.
Down to the water's edge,
Where I can slip in nice and slow.
Hope everyone has a great time,
And somehow finds the lake.
Cause is another hot day baking,
Out on this Georgia clay.....

My Journey

My journey has been a long one,
Many bumps along the way.
I've had some fun,
But boy have I paid.
My journey has many scars,
And oh the stories my songs tell.
From beautiful nights under the star's,
To nights of endless hell.
My journey brought me a lover,
Who became my wife.
Two daughters and a great son,
Was well worth all the strife.
My journey gave me many friends,
But around here I have like 3.
The rest are still playing songs,
In Nashville Tennessee.
My journey blessed me with 2 brothers,
I respect more than they'll ever know.
Especially after having my back,
When her true colors began to show.
My journey gave me grandparents,
Who gave me a devotion so strong.
Granny taught me humility,
Papa taught me to play songs.
My journey had stops at circle k,
To see folks who became friends.
Then became more like family,
Before the store came to an end.
My journey gave me the best neighbors,
That anyone could hope to meet.
34 years you are family,
And you're still across the street.
My journey gave me the gift to love,
And to give respect 'til it's abused.
But it also gave me 2 good feet,
To kick whoever I need too.
My journey has not been easy,
But rest assured my friend.
I'll go to my grave smiling,
When my journey reaches its end.....

Thank You To My Friend

The miles traveled behind me,
Lord the lunch was good.
With a woman I love dearly,
In her neck of the woods.

I enjoyed the riverside cafe,
I enjoyed our little talk.
I even enjoyed the steps we took,
When we took that walk.

One of the best friends I've ever had,
No drama no trouble no strife.
The one everybody thinks,
Has been my longtime wife.

Now I'm strapping up the guitar,
About to head back that way.
With miles traveled behind me,
Right where they need to stay...

Written by: Mitchell B Cooper
dedicated to Kayla Burdeshaw...
Thanks for the riverside lunch and walk....
I enjoyed the time.

Like A Bird

The young boy was a loner,
Music was his world.
It healed pain and suffering,
From illness, death, and girls.
Started with a piano,
As his papa taught him to play.
'Til like a bird,
He flew away....
On up to Nashville,
Chasing those dreams.
The young man had it all,
At least that's how it seemed.
But he missed his kids in Georgia,
So he packed on up one day.
Then like a bird,
He flew away.....
Like a bird he soared,
Up those music charts.
Writer of the year,
Writer of the heart.
He's written for many,
If you listen you've heard.
Songs of the man,
That's like a bird....
Now the years have caught him,
He's always in pain.
A daily fight with doctors,
Is now his biggest strain.
Just waiting 'til the day comes,
His name can be heard.
And with the angels he will fly,
Like a bird...
Like a bird in the blue sky,
Singing loud and clear.
Heavens New Angel,
Is a writer of the year.
He'll write away in heaven,
Through thunder he'll be heard.
Singing away,
Like a bird....
When judgement days upon him,
He'll get all the praise he deserves.
Then for eternity he'll sing,
Like a bird.....

Shinning My Boots

Shinning my boots,
Pressing my jeans.
It's in my roots,
This music thing.

Sang for some kids,
Wrote for a few.
The task is done did,
I was done by 2.

Now back home,
Melissa on line.
Thinking of a song,
Hopefully one of mine.

It's got a beat in my roots,
My soul knows what it means.
So I'm shining my boots,
And pressing my jeans....

If I Could

If I could I would be,
Up onstage somewhere.
If I could I would write,
Hit after hit I swear.

If I could I'd be a good father,
To those who are my world.
If I could I'd leave millions,
To my son and girls...

If I could I'd love a woman,
Who was faithful and true.
If I could I'd forget the past,
Of folks like you.

If I could I'd be smart like my brothers,
But for now I'll just write.
If I could I'd spoil grand babies,
In the Georgia sunlight.

If I could I'd be a friend,
To everyone in need.
If I could I'd be the one,
Planting hope as a seed.

If I could I'd sing loudly,
Even if I was no good.
Oh I'd love to just start over,
If I could.....

The Winding Path

Along the winding path, twisted in my dreams.
I go round and round forever, lost in time it seems.
I see visions all around, I hear the voices too.
So I found a seat, along the river in my view.

I could hear the water rolling, I could feel the cool breeze.
I could see the beauty from above, shining down through the trees.
I talked to God heart to heart, and listened to his reply.
Then I sat there so humble, as I began to cry.

My tears filled the stream, it was clear I was in pain.
That's when I heard a voice, calling out my name.
Then before my very eyes, Jesus was there upon the stream.
Reaching out his hand, forgiving everything.

I said father I'm far from perfect, but I love faithful and true.
Why is faithless all I find, and wrong is all I do.
Have I not prayed for strangers, have I not played for a sick child.
Have I not donated my money, have I not calmed the wild.

I just want what anyone should, true love and honesty.
That's when Jesus said my son, you'll only find that in me.
Today sinners run rampant, and they all must repent.
Before I go call the role, or to hell they will be sent.

Don't you worry about nobody, my son you'll be just fine.
With that Jesus rose on up, And disappeared into the sky.
I sat and for a moment, I felt the weight of my burdens unload.
I stood to my feet a New man, and recalled all I was told.

Yeah this morning when I woke, I was ready to unleash my wrath.
That is 'til I found Jesus,
Along the winding path....

He Came To Life Again

Down a long winding road, the man took walk.
He thought of what to say, so he and Jesus could talk.
He started with bless my family, and forgive me for my sins.
That's when,
He came to life again....

He walked on down the highway, a little farther down the road.
Talking away to Jesus, trying to ease his load.
The burden it was heavy, but he let it loose from within.
That's when,
He came to life again....

He came to life,
He jumped and screamed.
Lord thank you much,
For saving me.
He bowed his head,
He sat and cried.
With Jesus in his heart,
He came to life.....

The man yelled to the neighbors, said glory be thy name.
Some yelled with him, some turned away in shame.
That old man started yelling, Jesus, please save my friends.
That's when,
He came to life again.

He came to life,
He jumped and screamed.
Lord thank you much,
For saving me.
He bowed his head,
He sat and cried.
With Jesus in his heart,
He came to life.....

No the devil could not stop him,
No matter how hard he tried.
With Jesus in his heart,
He came to life........

From The Land Of Mere Forgottens

From the land of mere forgottens,
To the stages of the well-known.
A Lula poet poured out his heart,
In every poem and every song.
He wrote about better days,
Left buried in the past.
He wrote of loves that came,
And left way too fast.

From the land of mere forgottens,
People who believe in dreams.
Those that write day and night,
Songs that nobody sings.
In every city and every town,
He wrote about days back home.
Now that he's finally here,
He's ready to again be gone.

From the land of mere forgottens,
From Maysville and Lula, G..A.
There's a poem dedicated to you,
Wishing happiness All the way.
Cherish your memories before their dead,
Left tossed away and rotten.
Buried forever amidst the demons,
In the land of mere forgottens....

Just Two Roses

The man said "would you like to donate?" I said "what's it going for?"
He thought for just a minute...then honestly said "I'm not sure".
Shocked I said, "Why should I give...If you don't know where it goes".
The man said "the change goes to booze and the dollars go to a rose"....

I couldn't believe what the man had said, and I laughed just a little bit.
The man just looked and said "you asked...and buddy I don't fib."
"I may be just a low down bum...but my kids still are my world".
"So mister would you like to donate. So I can provide for myself and my girls"

I reached down and grabbed some cash...it wasn't much but it would do.
I said "I sure hope this helps"...he said "It will sir, and I thank you".
I drove off just thinking...I bet he spends it all on beer.
So I parked the car about 100 yards...so I could see where he went from there...

The man went straight to the liquor store...and came out with a little brown bag.
I just sat there thinking to myself...now that right there is sad.
He walked into another store...and came out with roses in paper.
He hollered back "I'll bring you the difference"...the owner said we'll settle later.

The man then walked about a mile down the road..passing names I've never known.
'Til he stopped real quick and took off his hat...then knelt down by a stone.
I could hear him talking on...but I couldn't hear what was said.
I could tell he was hurting...as tears flowed from eyes so red.

He hollered "I've given you my everything...why can't you take me home to them".
Then I watched the old man break down....as tears fell again and again.
After a while the old man got up..and started out my way.
I didn't have time to crank up, and I didn't know what to say.

As he approached me in my car... he said "you have brightened my world".
'Cause tonight there are 2 roses...lying next to my two girls"....
I can never repay...what you have done today....
The two roses were for my girls....

I Wasn't Thinking, I Was Drinking

The note there on the table…
Said "I don't understand.
You were once my prince charming,
A confident handsome man.
I don't know what changed;
What were you thinking?"
I wrote, "I wasn't thinking…
I was drinking…

With the first drink I got madder…
With the second I quietened down…
With the fifth I hit the dance floor…
And shook myself around…
So while you're bragging to your friends…
Saying "I wonder what he's thinking…..
Honey I wasn't thinking…
I was drinking…

I made up a new dance…
Even found one to dance along…
I got up on that stage…And even sung a song…
Yeah you broke my heart…
But the only thing here sinking…
Is that lime in my drink…
That I'm drinking…
With the sixth drink she got prettier…
With the tenth I was out the door….
Then one little shot of Bourbon…
We were laid out on her floor…
So if you're sitting around…
If our last light of love is blinking…
Just know I wasn't thinking…
I was drinking…

I left you the bill…
For what I was drinking…

The Rumor

From the shores of Jordon,
Across the Middle East.
The rumor of a coming,
Of an unseen beast.

Tales of horns and claws,
Echo across the land.
And visions of blood lost,
Scar every man.

From sea to shining sea,
The blood will flow.
From Israel to galilee,
There will be lost souls.

The angels have sounded,
Trumpets have been heard.
And facts have become unfounded,
By the spreading of false word.

The good book tells us clearly,
The Victor of the war.
Is the one who loves you dearly,
And all that you stand for.

So prepare yourself my brother,
And my sister too.
Before it is too late,
And the rumor becomes the truth.....

Barefoot Walk

On a barefoot walk…Across the sand.
In the scorching suns…No shade to stand.
The old man saw a vision…The heat was it playing games?
He wobbled just a little…Then fell in dizzying pain.

He took a few struggled breaths…He knew he was going to die.
So he turned his attention…To a power greater than you or I.
He uttered dear Lord Jesus…If you see me upon this sand.
I know I'm no saint…I'm a lost sinner man.

But Lord if you'll have me…I can feel you tugging my heart.
So please won't you enter…And give me a new start.
As he faded off in the heat…An Angel came below.
With a cool breeze he whispered…Child it's not your time to go.

GOD has jobs for you…You have work to do.
So rise up my son…This heat won't stop you.
Then as quick as he appeared…The Angel was gone.
But soon after came another…With a different and strange tone.

Saying why not lay on down…GOD don't care for you.
He left you in your time of need…There was nothing he could do.
So curse him and you'll feel better…Denounce him and you'll be well.
Or you could hold on to faith…And endure all this hell.

With that the Angel of death turned away…And before he could say another word.
A terrible thunder shook the heavens…And finally GOD was heard.
"My son rise up to your feet…Dust your cloak off.
Tell that devil you are mine…Be tough don't be soft.

Lean on me a little longer…My son if you'll look back.
They're in the sands below…Those are my tracks.
Through this dessert I've carried you…And I'll carry you some more.
Right across the holy land…To galilees shore.
Be strong son don't waver…Just have faith in me.
As this barefoot walk across the sand…Let's your burdened soul run free.

Little Umbrella

inspired by Sarah Ann

To Arkansas, From New York…
To that Lula, Georgia home.
The skies are growing dark…
A storm is coming on.
A beautiful lady awaits…
Even if I'm soaking wet.
But this little umbrella…
Is as good as it gets….

The first drop got me,
The second and third too.
That little umbrella,
Protected me from a few.
Still within the pouring rain,
I am soaking wet.
This little umbrella,
Is as good as it gets….

This little umbrella… Too small for a child.
Much less a grown woman…When the weather is wild.
It may shield me a little…Still I'm soaking wet.
This little umbrella,
Is as good as it gets….

No pictures of no princess,
Those days are gone.
Nowadays it's just solid colors,
Then again I'm grown.
So today here I am,
A day I won't forget.
When this little umbrella,
Is as good as it gets….

This little umbrella…Too small for a child.
Much less a grown woman…When the weather is wild.
It may shield me a little…But still I'm soaking wet.
This little umbrella,
Is as good as it gets……

Come rain or shine,
These days I won't forget.
When this little umbrella,
Is as good as it gets…..

The Waves

I sit alone on the shoreline,
Staring out to see…
The waves play the music,
In a slow melody.

I see blue skies forever,
I feel the Sun upon my face.
And I'm rocked to sleep gently,
By the never ending waves.

In the crash I hear a deep voice,
In my heart I know it well.
God was speaking to me,
While the waves all fell.

I heard children laughing,
I heard some who were in fear.
As the waves grew bigger,
Before they reached the pier.

It was peace I find no more,
Back home or any place.
But as I sit alone on the shoreline,
I found it in the waves....

Goodbye

On a cold and rainy night,
He lost his life on a bull named Desperado,
She got the hurtful news,
Of the love she'd hate to lose in Colorado,

She put his buckles on the shelf,
Like her heart the night he died,
She never thought she'd
Ever say goodbye.....

She raised him on her own,
To be a man when he came home from college,
He had the finest things in life,
He had a doctor for a wife,
And six years of knowledge,

She put his pictures on the shelf,
Like her heart the night she cried,
She never thought she'd
Ever say goodbye

He had a practice in Atlanta,
And a home down in Savannah,
The day she told him she would die,
She said don't cry no tears,
You were my joy throughout my years
But it's time for me to fly.

He put her ashes on the shelf,
Like his heart the day she died,
He never thought he'd
Ever say goodbye.......
Goodbye..........Goodbye........

He's My Dad

Ever since I was a boy,
My dad walked me through life
He's been there for everything
Even when I met my wife.
He filled me up with knowledge
So my light would never be dim
I wouldn't be the man I am today
If it hadn't been for him.

Through the times that were good
And the times that were bad
He's always been there for me,
He's my dad

I took his favorite drill apart
Just to see how it ran
I thought he would hate me
But he just took it like a man
I can't say he was happy
Seeing what I'd done
But he said he loved me anyway
And I was his only son

Through the times that were good
And the times that were bad
He's always been there for me,
He's my dad

Momma's Favorite Words

I've heard them before,
Directed at me.
But mostly at dad,
After all I'm only three.
She says they're to encourage,
Dad says they're to hurt.
They're my daily dreams,
Momma's favorite words.

Like "Do it now"
"Because I said so"
Or of course the infamous "no"
They're what I hear
When they need to be heard
They're not threats, they're promises.
Momma's Favorite words!

A daily "I love you"
To start off the day
A night time "sleep tight"
To keep the boogieman away
One my daddy gets from her
Every night somehow
When I'm nearly asleep,
I always hear "Not Now!"

They're mom's favorite words
"I love you" or "Get lost"
And of course when we're shopping
"Do you know how much that costs?
"I'm not made of money"
Lord the times that's been heard
They're tough but they're loving
Momma's favorite words

They're tough but they're loving
Momma's favorite words

Nashville Tennessee

I'VE HAD THE LIFE OF PLEASURE,
COMPARED TO MOST I KNOW.
THE LOVE AND SUPPORT OF GOOD FRIENDS,
WHO BELIEVED IN MY SONGS.
I'VE WRITTEN WITH GEORGIAS BEST,
AND TOOK THE LESSONS LEARNED WITH ME.
TO NASHVILLE, TENNESSEE.....

I WROTE WEDDING VOWS,
FOR THE WOMAN I LOVED.
I WROTE SONGS OF INSPIRATION,
INSPIRING OTTHERS TO NEVER GIVE UP.
I'VE EVEN TO THE ONE,
WHO'S BY MY SIDE IN EVERY DREAM.
ASKING PLEASE COME NORTII ON 24
TO NASHVILLE, TENNESSEE.....

TO NASHVILLE TENNNESSEE,
AMIDST ALL THE STARS AND LIGHTS
I WOULD LOVE HOLD YOU CLOSE TO ME,
AND LOVE YOU ALL THROUGH THE NIGHT.
IF YOU EVER LEAVE GEORGIA.
I HOPE YOU KNOW YOU'RE STILL WITH ME,
YOU'RE IN MY HEART, MY PRAYERS, AND MY THOUHGTS,
UP IN NASHVILLE, TENNSSEE.........

I'VE HAD THE CHANCE TO MOVE ON,
BUT I'VE CHOSEN TO STAY BEHIND.
MY BODY'S MOVED ON TO WRITE MY SONGS,
BUT I LEFT MY HEART, SOUL, AND MIND.
SOMEDAY SOON I PRAY THERE'S A KNOCK,
AND THROUGH MY DOORSPEEP HOLE I'LL SEE.
THE LULA WOMAN WHO HOLDS MY HEART AND SOUL,
HAS COME NORTH TO NASHVILLE TENNSSEE.

TO NASHVILLE TENNESSEE,
I WOULD LOVE TO SHOW YOU THE STARS.
HAVE ANIGHT WITH YOU CLOSE TO ME,
SHARING MOMENTS HEART TO HEART.
IF YOU NEVER LEAVE GEORGIA,
I HOPE YOU KNOW YOU'RE STILL WITH ME.
YOU'RE IN MY HEART, MY PRAYERS.MY THOUGHTS,
UP IN NASHVILLE, TENNESSE.......
YOU'RE IN MY IIEART, IN MY PRAYERS, IN MY THOUGHTS,
UP IN NASHVILLE TENNESSEE...

Nashville's Finest

No appreciation,
For a job well done
For some of Nashville's finest
Daughters and sons
It's a long hard road
Filled with danger and hate
God bless you and thanks

For being a protector
When our defenses are down
For being a helper
When we're lost in town
For being an enforcer
Of the laws we have today
It's time we stand up and say to you all
To Nashville's finest,
Please be safe

No pat on the back
For changing a life
Of a lonesome homeless man
You showed respect for tonight
It's a job for the few
The proud and the brave
It's because of you
Nashville's at its finest today

You're a sworn protector
Doing a fine job
Of helping your fellow neighbor
When his dreams get robbed
You're the peace of mind for us all
At the end of every day
To Nashville's finest
Please be safe

To Nashville's finest
May God keep you safe

Queen Of Broken Hearts

SHE HOLDS THE KEY
THAT UNLOCKS HIS HEART
WITH BROKEN DOWN DREAMS BEHIND HER
HER WORLD HAS COME APART
AS SHE GOES THRU LIFE
JUST LIVIN' DAY BY DAY
SHE REFLECTS BACK ON THE LOVE
THAT HE NEVER GAVE AWAY

SHE HOLDS THE KEY TO THE MAIL BOX
SHE HOLDS THE KEY TO HIS HEART
SHE WAS THE ONE WHO TORE…HIS WORLD APART
SHE BECAME THE QUEEN OF BROKEN HEARTS…

SHE PICKS UP THE PIECES
TRIES TO MOVE ON
THINKS ABOUT THEIR MEMORIES
NOW THAT HE'S GONE
SHE TRYS TO COVER UP THE TEARS
THAT WON'T GO AWAY
SHE BECAME THE QUEEN OF BROKEN HEARTS
OF A LOVE THAT COULDN'T BE SAVED

SHE HOLDS THE KEY TO THE MAIL BOX
SHE HOLDS THE KEY TO HIS HEART
SHE WAS THE ONE WHO TORE…HIS WORLD APART
SHE BECAME THE QUEEN OF BROKEN HEARTS…

IN HER MIND SHE LOOKS BACK
ON THE LOVE SHE GAVE AWAY
AS HE TOOK IT WITH HIM
'TIL HIS DYING DAY
SHE'S THE QUEEN OF BROKEN HEARTS
IN A WORLD THAT'S COME APART
SHE'S THE QUEEN OF BROKEN HEARTS
IN A WORLD THAT'S COME APART

Sea Of White Crosses

Standing on the hill looking out
Across the field where they lay
The bugler playing taps
As another soldier takes his place
It's sad but yet it's an honor
To be amongst this field with all its losses
It's amazing the peace that I feel
Looking out at a sea of white crosses

A sea of white crosses
Engraved with many names
From those who died as heroes
To those who were slain
It's a place where America
Counts up her many losses
It's Arlington cemeteries
Sea of white crosses

Today they laid one more down
He finally came home from Iraq
He swore when he left this town
Someday he would be back
Today he took his place
At the throne of heaven's bosses
As they laid his body to rest
Amongst the sea of white crosses

Standing At The Crossroads

Here I am in the morning
Standing at the crossroads in life
Guitar in my hand
A country born man
Trying to live right

I see the light up ahead
At the crossroads in life
Directing the flow
Of where I go
When I see the light

I'm standing at the crossroads
Which way do I go
Take a left into another bar
Or take a right and go home
It's a crowded intersection
That needs a light
I'm standing at the crossroads
In life

The devil's staring me down
So I need to hold on tight
To all the things I love
If I wanna see the light

The Wheel

THE WHEEL WAS ROLLING
SPINING ROUND AND ROUND
I WAS ON DECK WITH A MILLER LITE
TIL I HIT THE GROUND.

TWO LONELY ANGELS BESIDE ME,
ONE MORE ON THE FLOOR.
SO WHY IN THE HELL AM I,
GETTIN' THROWN OUT THE DOOR.

BARTENDER TELL EM TO LEAVE ME ALONE,
I STILL HAVE ANOTHER SIP...
I'M A PAYIN' PATRON OF THE WHEEL,
SO WHY AM I SITIN" ON THE STRIP.

THE WHEEL WAS A ROCKIN",
THE BAND WAS BANGIN' OUT HITS.
NO MILLER LITE LEFT TO DRINK,
AND I NEED TO WET MY LIPS.

SO I MADE MY WAY TO THE BAR,
PUSHED ON THE DANCE FLOOR.
NOW WOULD SOMEONE PLEASE TELL ME,
WHY I'M GETTIN' THROWN OUT THE DOOR

BARTENDER TELL EM TO LEAVE ME ALONE,
I STILL HAVE ANOTHER SIP...
I'M A PAYIN' PATRON OF THE WHEEL,
SO WHY AM I SITIN" ON THE STRIP.

JUST ANOTHER NIGHT ON SECOND AVENUE
BEIN' A PATRON OF THE WHEEL.....LIKE YOU

Across The County Line

TRAVELING DOWN THE ROAD TONIGHT,
I'VE GOT YOU ON MY MIND.
THINKIN' ABOUT YOUR LOVE FOR ME,
AND WHAT I'VE LEFT BEHIND.
AS I'M HEADED BACK YOUR WAY AGAIN
I'M REACHIN' THE COUNTY LINE
TRYIN' TO GET BACK TO YOU, AND YOUR LOVE
A DAY AHEAD OF TIME

SHE DOES EVERYTHING I ASK OF HER,
HER DEMEANOR IS PLEASANT AND WARM.
SHE'S BEEN I THERE IN THAT SMALL TOWN,
EVER SINCE THE DAY SHE WAS BORN.
I HAVE MET A FEW OTHERS
THEY'VE COME AND GONE
BUT SHE'S BEEN HERE FOR ME.... ALL ALONG

SO TONIGHT WE'RE GONNA MAKE LOVE
UP UNTIL THE DAWN
DISCUSS WHERE WE'D LEFT OFF
AND WHAT HAD GONE WRONG
MAYBE THERE'LL COME A DAY
WHEN WE WON'T BE APART
WE JUST NEED TO FIND AWAY
TO FIND IT IN OUR HEARTS

SHE DOES EVERYTHING I ASK OF HER,
HER DEMEANOR IS PLEASANT AND WARM.
SHE'S BEEN I THERE IN THAT SMALL TOWN,
EVER SINCE THE DAY SHE WAS BORN.
I HAVE MET A FEW OTHERS
THEY'VE COME AND GONE
BUT SHE'S BEEN HERE FOR ME.... ALL ALONG

I HOPE WE CAN DO THIS
I HOPE THERE 'LL COME A DAY.
THAT WE CAN BOTH LISTEN,
SOMEWHERE ALONG THE WAY.
CAUSE IF IT'S MEANT TO BE,
THERE'LL COME A TIME.
THOUGH I CAN'T GET YOU OFF MY MIND,
AS I'M CROSSIN'G THE COUNTY LINE

If You Don't Know

If you don't know giving your last dollar,
To a stranger who needs a meal.
If You don't know what it's like,...
It's sad that most never will.
If you don't know donating your time,
Playing songs you wrote for kids.
If You don't know what it's like,
It's a blessing to be like this.

If you don't know how to lend a hand,
To someone needing help.
Then You don't know what it's like,
To truly be proud of yourself.
If you don't know what it's like,
To love all and always forgive.
I feel sorry for that burden,
You must deal with as you live.

If you don't know how to love true,
Without lies, and deceit.
I hope your eyes are opened wide,
When true love is laid right at your feet.
If you don't know a humble heart,
And it's your way and nothing else.
You need to take a step back,
And take a good look at yourself.

If you don't know God above,
I pray soon that his grace shows.
And I wish you all nothing but love,
Especially if you don't know....

Santa Can You Hear Me

Santa can you hear me,
Do you help the homeless too?
Mama says she's trying,
But we barely have any food.
My brother is only 1,
And I myself I'm 3.
So all I want for Christmas,
Is a home for my family...
Santa can you hear me,
I know at times I've been bad.
But my brother hasn't did 1 thing,
And to see him suffer makes me sad.
I know that mama's trying,
And she says you'll get this letter.
So all I want for Christmas Santa,
Is for you to make it all better.
Santa can you hear me,
If so please know I'll be looking out.
I'll be keeping the faith,
'Til I hear you holler and shout.
On Dasher on Dancer,
On Prancer, on Vixen.
On Comet, on Cupid,
On Donner, on Blitzen.
Santa I will listen close,
And I'm sure Rudolph is a sight to see.
Please just give me a sign,
Santa can you hear me......

Waiting On You

Today I woke…and there was no pain.
I saw dad and my brothers…and I hugged them all again.
We spent last evening on a cloud…looking down watching over you.
We'll be right here waiting…when your job on Earth is through.

Mama, don't cry…be happy and rejoice.
God's a fan of the Blalocks…and the credit is all yours.
If you feel sad just close your eyes…and you'll see us at Heaven's Gate.
Just waiting on you…Yes mama, you're well worth the wait.

Today we all went fishing…and sat out on the shore.
We caught and we caught…'til we couldn't carry no more.
We had church in the morning…and sang in perfect tune.
God says, "That Choir leader's spot…"Well mama, it's reserved for you.

Mama, don't cry…be happy and rejoice.
God's a fan of the Blalocks…and the credit is all yours.
If you feel sad just close your eyes…and you'll see us at Heaven's Gate.
Just waiting on you…Yes mama, you're well worth the wait.

Can't wait to see your smile,
We'll be waiting for you,
Just inside of Heaven's Gate….
Waiting on You

Inspired by the strongest woman who will ever live…
I Love you Aunt Cricket

The Walk

Left foot right foot left again,
As I get on down the road.
I have nothing to do or no friends,
So walking I shall go.
Around my town a few miles,
Taking in the scenes.
I'll be back in a little while,
Unless death catches me.

I'm taking the walk nobody wants,
It's long lonely and cold.
The suns went down its dark outside,
Still I must go.
I'm taking the walk pass the ballpark,
Covered in graffiti and colored chalk.
Nothing left to do so I'm telling you,
I'm gone to take the walk...

Inhale exhale inhale again,
These hills seem bigger these days.
Still I bare it all with a grin,
And continue on my way.
Up and down around and around,
All over these Lula streets.
It's time to explore this town,
Unless death catches me.

I'm taking the walk nobody wants,
It's long lonely and cold.
The suns went down I should be inside,
Man I'm getting old.
I'm taking the walk pass the ballpark,
Covered in graffiti and chalk.
Nothing left to do so I'm telling you,
I'm gone to take a walk....

There's nothing left to do but that's nothing new,
So I'm gone to take a walk.....

Down A Long Winding Path

Down a long winding path…the man went one day.
He was looking for salvation…and a calming place to pray.
He came up on a river…water rushing bye.
And he thought to himself…this is a good place to write.
He sat there all alone…a notebook and his thoughts.
He wrote and he wrote…oh the lessons nature taught.

He wrote about his dear wife…and how he missed her by his side.
He wrote about his kids…the best gifts of his life.
He wrote about that special aunt…who held a special place in his heart.
He wrote about his music…his poetry and his art.

He sat there all day long…just nature at its best.
No construction going on…no congested mess.
He talked a bit to Jesus…pouring out his heart.
Thanking him for his blessings…in the life he'd torn apart.

He said lord I know I've failed you…but I'm trying my very best.
I still get lost along the way…I still fail the test.
If you'll have me…beaten battered and bruised.
Then lord I would like…to devote my life to you.

Through the clouds came a rumble…and there through the trees.
There came a voice like no other…in a mid-summer breeze.
Saying son I've got your name down…I will see you someday soon.
But for now they're poems to write…and things to do.

There's a lady up the highway…you need to take to dinner again.
There's children that need a daddy…who can double as a friend.
There's a granddaughter that's so awesome…that you just can't resist.
Every time she's around…to somehow steal a kiss.

Enjoy the gifts I've given…and you shall never feel my wrath.
That's the lessons to take with you…as you head back up the path.

The Night Time Is Calling

The night time is calling,
but the sun is still up.
Warming my drink,
in my solo cup.

I'm sitting and writing,
nothing else to do.
Maybe I'll come up,
with a song or two.

In the meantime its poems,
while I rock away.
Still hungover,
from my 2 days at the stage.

Cold drinks beside me,
notebook in hand.
It's a pretty good life,
for a simple man.

So come rock with me,
stay for a while.
We'll have a few laughs,
and share a few smiles.

It's time to relax,
and just sit out and rock.
The night time is calling,
ready or not....

Is That You

Is that you sneaking in,
Peeking through my blinds.
Go away Thursday you're no friend,
At least no friend of mine.

Is that you pushing away,
My sleep and sanity.
Let me stay at least 'til 8,
Go away don't bother me.

Is that you causing those birds,
To sing loud and clear.
Yes it's a song I've heard,
Still it brings me to tears.

Is that you lighting up this room,
A little more and more with time.
It will be daylight soon,
That should be a crime.

Is that you pushing me,
Saying I've got things to go and do.
All I want, all I need,
Is to know is that you????

All My Life

All of my life…my Music's led the way…
I memorized…Every song that I hear play…
I've been through struggles….And I've seen the strife…
But music's led the way…
All of my life…

All of my life…I've played out all my dreams…
Every note of my future…Is in these guitar strings…
From my first loves, my first kid….And my first wife….
Yes my music's led the way….
All of my life…

All of my life….All of my 42 years….
In all I write….In every salty little tears…
I've seen the better things…I've lived up on high…
And my music's led the way…
All of my life…

All of my life…I've dreaded the coming days…
When the times…start taking folks away….
They'll gather round…Just to tell me goodbye
Music will lead the way….
Like all my life

All my life…All of my 42 years…
In all I write….In every Icy cold beer…
I've seen the better things…I've lived up on high….
And my music's led the way…
All of my life….

Yeah, I've seen better things…I've lived up on high…
Music's led the way…All of my life…

Into A Song

Over in the corner,
Tucked away alone.
Having a little dinner,
While waiting on a song.
So I gathered up my senses,
And let the night lead me on.
As life faded away…Into a song.

It wasn't fast…
Nor was it slow.
Just the perfect setting,
To a perfect song.
I mentioned her beauty…
She mentioned my cologne.
As life faded away….Into a song…

Into a song….Casting away all fears…
The music make me strong…
Even if the lyrics bring me tears…
A simple lyrical genius…
It's what keeps me keeping on…
As life fades away….Into a song…

As singers come and go,
And I write a way.
One thing I know,
One thing I'll say.
If I die don't you cry…
My life's been good and long,
So let me fade away…Into a song…

Into a song…casting away all fears…
The music makes me strong…
While the lyrics bring me to tears…
A simple lyrical Genius…
It's what keeps me keeping on…
As life fades away….Into a song…

Glory Days

At this old age…I'm writing away…
Through the smoke and the beer.
Writing my songs…The singing along…
From this bar room chair.

Tapping my toes…To every note…
As the music plays.
In what I live for…In this bar…
Reliving my glory days.

Glory Days of my past…Passing bye really fast…
Memories are gone…In my songs…
And every country hit.
Glory days in these bars….Damn right set in my ways…
Passing the night…Beneath the light…
Of those glory days…

Lead me on….back to my home…
Put on another stage.
Out in that spotlight…For another night…
Reliving my glory days.

Glory Days of my past…Passing bye really fast…
Memories are gone…In my songs…
And every country hit,
Glory days in these bars….Damn right set in my ways…
Passing the night…Beneath the light…
Of those glory days…

I'm just passing the nights…
Beneath the lights…
Of those glory days…

Live At The Bar

Live at the bar…
Straight from the heart…
Songs from me to you.
Beneath these faded lights…
I find a corner to write…
Songs that are true.

Live at the bar…
Smoking a Cuban cigar…
I come alive in these songs.
Singer to singer…
I'm a songwriting ringer…
Live at the bar back home.

No last calls….
Cowboys with balls…
And the ladies give all their heart.
That's how it goes…
When I'm back home…
Live at the Bar.

Live at the Bar…
Karaoke with no guitars…
'Til the last lady goes home.
Back to the house…
Songs playing loud…
'Til the memories are gone.

No last calls…
Cowboys with balls…
And the ladies give all their heart.
That's how it goes…
When I'm back home…
Live at the Bar.

That's just how it goes…
When I'm back home…
Coming live at the Bar

This Guitar And Me

From the first drop tonight,
Out beneath those lights,
Standing in the Georgia Rain.
I listened to the crowd,
Singing out loud,
Erasing all of my Pain.

Note after Note,
In the songs we wrote,
For once I was free.
Finally alive,
In those stage lights,
Just this guitar and Me.

This guitar and me,
How it's meant to be,
Helping me along.
How it's meant to be,
This Guitar, Me,
And a new Song.

Up here onstage,
Playing my worries away,
Finally feeling Free.
Helping me along,
Was a new Song,
This Guitar and Me.

This guitar and me,
How it's meant to be,
Helping me along.
How it's meant to be,
This Guitar, Me,
And a new Song.

That's how it's meant to be,
Between this Guitar and Me.

On The Road

I've been on the road…
Sooo damn long.
I forgot how home feel…
The stage and the lights.
Every night…
From LA to Nashville.

I've passed the miles…
I've shared some smiles…
I've carried a heavy load.
But when they ask…
Where my time is passed…
I tell'em I've been on the road.

I've been on the road…
In towns I don't know…
Singing and writing my life away.
You can believe what you're told…
That I've been on the road…
Listening to those bands play.

Through that bus glass…
I watch the miles pass…
Getting me everywhere I need to go.
'Til I have to tell 'em again…
Where I've been…
When I've been on the road….

I've been on the road…
In towns I don't know…
Singing and writing my life away.
You can believe what you're told…
That I've been on the road…
Listening to those bands play.

Believe what you're told…My life is on the road…
Listening to those bands play…

I Don't Care

Don't care about your money…
Don't care about your fame.
I'm looking for the one…
Who has her own "Name".

Don't care about no mansion…
Don't care what you drive.
I'm looking for the one…
Who makes me feel Alive.

Yes, I hear you talking,
I've heard all you said.
I'm not gonna be a retirement fund,
For you when I'm dead.
Call me mean if you must,
I won't shed a tear.
If that offends you,
I don't care…

Don't care if you're single,
Don't care if you're fine.
I'm looking for the one,
Not looking for a dime.
Don't care about your fortune,
Don't care if you're broke.
I'm looking for the one,
Who's not a Joke.

Yes, I hear you talking,
I've heard all you said.
I'm not gonna be a retirement fund,
For you when I am Dead.
Call me mean if you must,
I won't shed a tear.
If that offends you,
I don't care…

Suck it up buttercup…Dry up your own tear
If that offends you…I Don't Care!!!

Defenders Of The Usa

War after War,
From shore to shore,
Through rockets and red glare.
The Bullets flew,
For the Red, White, and Blue,
Cruising through the air.

Defenders of Freedom,
We always need them,
From the past 'til today.
Standing strong,
For us back home,
Here in the USA.

God Bless the Vets,
America's Best,
Defenders in every way.
The one's we owe,
For the freedoms we know,
God Bless the Defenders of the USA.

Iraq to Afghanistan,
We've lost many a man,
Chasing Evil away…
'Til they all come home,
Where they belong,
The defenders of the USA.

God Bless the Vets,
America's Best,
Defenders in every way.
The one's we owe,
For the freedoms we know,
God Bless the Defenders of the USA.

They're the ones we owe,
For the freedoms we know,
The Defenders of the USA.

Pray For Us Too

(A Welcome Home Tribute)

I wish you a merry Christmas…And a happy New Year too.
While you're sitting 'round with family…I would like to ask a favor of you.
My name is sergeant Bentsen…I'm serving you here in Iraq.
I ask that you pray for my family…
'Cause they're all praying I'll be back.

Yes, those new stories are scary…But they'll never bring it to you live.
But stuck in sand with blood on your hands…Watching your best friend die.
So tonight when you bow your heads…I ask one small favor of you.
Pray for health, pray for the hungry…
But please…pray for us too!

Pray for us too…Trust me we need it out here.
We need to hear from you…To know you still care.
Tell me we're not forgotten…Tell me that I'm wrong.
Yes all I want for Christmas…
Is for you to tell me…welcome home!

I've got a buddy from high school…Run track in those days.
Who's coming home tomorrow…With his legs blown away.
And remember Mr. Nichols…The one who made everyone laugh?
Well He'll be home on Tuesday…
In a zipped up body bag!

So I'm asking you honey…And all Americans around.
To pray for your soldiers… 'Cause we're getting shot down.
It doesn't seem like much…But it's the most you can do.
When you bow your heads to pray tonight…
Please, pray for us too!

Pray for us too…Trust me we need it out here.
We need to hear from you…To know you still care.
Tell me we're not forgotten…Tell me that I'm wrong.
Yes all I want for Christmas,
Is for you to tell me…welcome home!

Pray for us too! Yeah pray for us too!

~Dedicated to America's brave sons & daughters who face death daily
So we can remain the free country we all know and love.
God Bless You…Merry Christmas…Be Safe…
Come Home Soon…We Miss You…We Love You!!!

How The Shoe Fits

When the night comes calling,
And you're all alone.
When all that's on your line,
Is that lonely dial tone,
That's when you will know,
How the shoe fits…
When the alarm goes off,
And nobody shuts it up.
When you yell for your coffee,
And he doesn't bring your cup.
That's when you will know,
How the shoe fits…

That's when you will know, whether it's an 8, 9, or 10.
That's when your heart, Will reach for me again.
That just one more minute that you like to take.
Will disappear in time, when nobody has to wait.
When that time comes, and you're ready to quit,
That's when you'll know, how the shoe fits…

When your head is hurting,
But the kids are all at home.
When you want to be romanced,
But find you're all alone.
That's when you will know,
How the shoe fits…

That's when you will know, whether it's an 8, 9, or 10.
That's when your heart, Will reach for me again.
That just one more minute that you like to take.
Will disappear in time, when nobody has to wait.
When that time comes, and you're ready to quit,
That's when you'll know, how the shoe fits…

When that time comes,
And you're ready to quit.
That's when you will know,
How the shoe fits.
Yeah that's when you will know,
How the shoe fits

Just Wait

You're always saying,
That I'm in a hurry for everything.
If I'd have patience,
You know it would pay off.
You always complain,
About me and my ways.
How I never take a stand,
How I'm too sort……..

Just wait! …Better days are coming,
They're just around the bend.
Just hold…On to your horses,
It will soon be great again.
Just wait…And I promise you,
A renewed trust of fate.
Better days are coming.
Just wait!

You say there's nothing left,
For you to love anymore.
How you notice,
That I no longer care.
You say your mind is set,
This time,
You're leaving for sure.
And you can't take it,
No more around here.

Just wait! …Better days are coming,
They're just around the bend.
Just hold…On to your horses,
It will soon be great again.
Just wait…And I promise you,
A renewed trust of fate.
Better days are coming.
Just wait!

Honey better days are coming…….
Just wait!!!

All Is Good All Is Well

Lately I try and try…To no avail.-
I wonder to myself…Why must I endure this hell.
Then they come crashing in…Saying daddy he did this again.
That's when I know…All is well…

Today it seems…Was like all others.
Sitting and wondering…Why do I bother.
Then the words ring loud…Daddy I need some help.
That's when I knew,…All is well…

All is well, all is good,
I wish they would stay the same.
All is well, in the neighborhood,
No criminals to take the blame.
So let's enjoy the moment, while it's here.
Oh, the stories we'll live to tell.
'Cause tonight, all is good, all is well…

Tomorrow the sun will rise,
Waking me with its glare.
I may wake with tears in my eyes,
'Cause I know that you're not here.
Then I'll hear footsteps in the hall,
And the smile will tell the tale.
Around here all is good,
All is well…

All is well, all is good,
I wish they would stay the same.
All is well, in the neighborhood,
No criminals to take the blame.
So let's enjoy the moment, while it's here.
Oh, the stories we'll live to tell.
'Cause tonight, all is good, all is well…

Around here all is good,
All is well…
Yeah all is well…

To Whom It May Concern

Today started like all others,
With me wanting to write.
Trying to find a subject,
That Nashville might like.
Then I saw a CMT Special,
Saying just do it your own way.
So Nashville,
There's something I need to say.

To whom it may concern,
This letter is meant for you.
You better not ignore us unheard ofs',
Remember at one time, you were like that too.
You better take time to read our lines,
Before somebody else takes your turn.
This letter is meant for you,
To whom it may concern…

Independent labels have sent me letters,
And the acknowledgments are piling up.
Still it shouldn't take a rocket scientist,
To figure out this stuff.
You need lyrics we need singers,
And it's always been that way.
So Nashville,
There's something I need to say.

To whom it may concern,
This letter is meant for you.
You better not ignore us unheard ofs',
Remember at one time, you were like that too.
You better take time to read our lines,
Before somebody else takes your turn.
This letter is meant for you,
To whom it may concern…

Take a chance,
You never know the money you could earn.
This letter is for you all,
To whom it may concern…

Copyright This

You said it was a waste of money,
When I filed that copyright.
It could've been spent on something useful,
Perhaps, something that you liked.
You left with all your packed up clothes,
'Til you heard my song's a "Hit".
Now you're sorry, you want to come back,
Well baby…copyright this…

Print it out on your copier,
Where you can see that finger good.
Blow it up on poster boards,
To hang throughout the neighborhood.
I begged you to stay when you left,
Still I was one person you'd never miss.
So do me a favor baby,
Copyright this!

You read all of my writings,
Never once found one you liked.
Instead you'd blow it off,
And fade into the night.
You walked away that summer night,
After ripping up my publishers' list.
Now you're sorry, you want to come back,
Well baby…copyright this…

Print it out on your copier,
Where you can see that finger good.
Blow it up on poster boards,
To hang throughout the neighborhood.
I begged you to stay when you left,
Still I was one person you'd never miss.
So do me a favor baby,
Copyright this!

Yeah print it out,
Nice and big,
Then go…
Copyright this!

Lost Cause

It's a lost cause…to even try.
A lost love…that you've let die.
I lost trust…you lost faith,
In those vows,
That we had made.
Nobody's to blame…it's nobody's fault.
Chalk it up…
To a lost cause…

Lost causes…will find you,
Throughout your life…
You'll sit alone…and think,
Why should I try?
No matter…what I do,
Her heart's been bought…
So I'll just…chalk it up,
To a lost cause!

A lost cause…or memory.
A lost picture…of our family.
I lost hope…you lost weight.
Weighing you down…
From bigger things…
Nobody's to blame…it's nobody's fault.
Chalk it up…
To a lost cause…

Lost causes…will find you,
Throughout your life…
You'll sit alone…and think,
Why should I try?
No matter…what I do,
Her heart's been bought…
So I'll just…chalk it up,
To a lost cause!

Yes I'll chalk it up,
To a lost cause…

The Man On My Wall

I see him every day,
But we never talk;
I don't guess we ever will…
I see me in his face,
And the way he stood and walked;
I'm a spitting image of him…
Now I wonder to myself,
If he can see me;
Or hear me when I talk…
I hope that he knows,
What he means to me;
He's not just a picture on my wall…

Lord they all must think that I'm crazy,
For talking to him the way that I do.
Tell me that he can see my babies,
And he knows what I'm going through.
I ask of you just one favor,
It's not really much at all.
When this body is done with its labor,
Can I meet the man on my wall…

I've heard that I have his demeanor,
How I'm so caring of others;
That I don't know…
You know that I'm not a big believer,
But my mother;
Even tells me that it's so…

Lord they all must think I'm crazy,
For talking to him like I do.
Tell me he can see my babies,
And he knows what I'm going through.
I ask of you just one favor,
It's not really much at all.
When this body is done with its labor,
Can I meet the man on my wall…

When I'm done with life's labor,
Can I meet the man on my wall…

Bring Daddy Home

Is that one there my present,
Is daddy coming back this year...
Santa promised he wouldn't forget,
When I whispered my wish in his ear.
I'm sure he's heard it all,
But as he said to me "I'll try".
I swear that Santa Claus,
Had a tear in his eyes...

Santa bring daddy home,
From that foreign land.
He swore he wouldn't be long,
After the fall of the Taliban.
I've really been good this year,
So my list is complete.
All I want for Christmas Santa,
Is my daddy home with me...

Mama has been doing good,
At least that's how it seems.
She saved all of our box scores,
We're the champions of the little league.
I know that she is sad and lonely,
But Santa I know you'll hear my prayers.
When Christmas morning comes at our house,
Please tell me that my daddy will be here.

Santa bring daddy home,
From that foreign land.
He swore he wouldn't be long,
After the fall of the Taliban.
I've really been good this year,
So my list is complete.
All I want for Christmas,
Is daddy home with me....

Santa all I want for Christmas,
Is my daddy home with me.....

Snow Birds Of January

Christmas has passed,
New years is gone.
All of those new songs,
Are getting old.
What a way to start,
That same old routine…..
The children with their mother,
The weekends are gone too fast.
I've forgotten memories,
I was hoping would last.
I don't guess,
Anything could make me happy…

Then those snowbirds of January,
Came tap tapping at my door.
I watch them fly so graceful in the sky,
'Til my worries aren't so big anymore.
If it wasn't for their presence,
I'd have to plead insanity.
Instead I watch them fly so graceful in the sky,
Those snowbirds of January….

Well my birthday is Friday,
Their mother of course has made plans.
So I sit here by myself,
On my piece of land.
It's my escape,
From this reality….
I feel the weight of the world,
Crushing me down.
I'm looking but I don't see,
Any help around.
I don't guess,
Anything could make me happy…

Then those snowbirds of January,
Came tap tapping at my door.
I watch them fly so graceful in the sky,
'Til my worries aren't so big anymore.
If it wasn't for their presence,
I'd have to plead insanity.
Instead I watch them fly so graceful in the sky,
Those snowbirds of January.

Mississippi Will Rise

Thousands lost in an instant,
I saw it all on my TV.
I've heard the cost up in the billions,
I know the folks and they know me.
I ask you neighbor,
For a hand.
To wipe the tears from just two eyes.
As we labor in the sand,
We'll conquer fear and Mississippi will rise…

From Biloxi to those gulf shores,
Of our neighbor over in Alabaam…
We'll come together yeah we'll endure,
Mississippi will rise before the sun goes down..

Off in the distance I can hear sobbing,
From all the people who lost everything.
I've heard of raping I've seen the robbing,
When we catch those folks well I hope they swing.

From Biloxi to those gulf shores,
Of our neighbor over in Alabaam..
We'll come together yeah we'll endure,
Mississippi will rise before the sun goes down…

Mississippi will rise before the sun goes down….

Won't You Give

(tribute to Egleston Children's Hospital)

Sometimes we find a cure,
For incurable stuff;
That's when a life is saved…
Sometimes we face death,
But we don't give up;
Be stern and keep the faith…
I've walked the hallways,
Of children's hospitals;
From Emory to Egleston…
It could make a grown man cry,
All the machines and needles;
If only we could just save one…

So please won't you give,
Spare just one dollar.
Help a child live through a day,
And get too tomorrow.
That's all we ask,
Is the chance to live.
Please want you help,
Want you give???

Sometimes we curse,
A hard workday;
Thinking our lives are coming undone.
While they bravely push on,
Through all the pain;
Our little daughters and sons…

So please won't you give,
Spare just one dollar.
Help a child live through a day,
And get too tomorrow.
That's all we ask,
Is the chance to live.
Please want you help,
Want you give???

Please won't you help,
Won't you give???

That When I Knew

She said sit down, we need to talk.
Please just listen, don't get up and walk.
I'm in love, with someone new.
That's when I knew, we were through...

She told me she was sorry, and I agreed.
For the pain, she was causing me.
I wished her luck, with someone new.
That's when I knew, we were through...

That's when I knew, we were through.
There was nothing else, that I could say or do.
I whispered to her, I still love you.
That's when I knew, we were through....

She "I've tried, to rule it out.
But his love, Leaves no doubts.
You're in my heart, I still love you.
That's when I knew, we were through.

That's when I knew, we were through.
There was nothing else, that I could say or do.
I whispered to her, I still love you.
That's when I knew, we were through....

What's ...when I knew,
We were through......

She's There With Me

Hey woman come here,
There's something on TV.
A rodeo in Saint Clair,
That's the one I wanted to see.
Even though I'm lying;
She's still there with me....

Hey woman where you going,
Would you like for me to go.
To the laundry mat or grocery store,
I don't really need to know.
As long as she's there with me,
I hope this time goes by slow....

When she is with me,
Lord I'm in the clouds.
As long as she is near me,
Can't nothing bring me down.
I hope she knows I love her,
I hope my love is clear to see.
There's nothing I cannot do,
As long as she is there with me...

Hey woman how are you feeling,
Was the workday rough on you.
There's something on the table,
Someone special sent to you.
Even though she's there with me,
Dinner and flowers alone will never do...

Hey woman do you want to cuddle,
Could I hold you in my arms.
What's that your head hurts,
Well don't worry there is no harm.
As she's there with me,
Lord delay that morning alarm...

When she is with me,
Lord I'm in the clouds.
As long as she is near me,
Can't nothing bring me down.
I hope she knows I love her,
I hope my love is clear to see.
There's nothing I cannot do,
As long as she is there with me...

No there's nothing I cannot do...When she is there....

Let Me Fly Free

I'd like to be included,
In my wife's every plan.
I'd like to be involved,
Like her husband…her man!
I don't know why she does it,
Sometimes I don't believe she cares.
She ignores me…the one and only man,
Who's always been there…

So lord I'm calling to you,
If I can get your number right.
I'm not a man of religion,
I haven't been all my life.
I'm tired of waiting on her,
If she's never going to see.
So if she loves someone new,
Let me fly free.

I'd like to be home,
With her every night.
When I'm here she is gone,
I no longer wonder why.
I don't know who stole her heart,
The one that swore she'd always care.
But I know it's a lot for me,
The one who's always been there…

So lord I'm calling to you,
If I can get your number right.
I'm not a man of religion,
I haven't been all my life.
I'm tired of waiting on her,
If she's never going to see.
So if she loves someone ncw,
Let me fly free…

No I know I'm not the one,
So let me fly free…

I See The Way

Mister I don't know your name,
I need to make this clear.
I made a promise 5 years ago today,
When only me and her were here.
She use to smile when I got home,
Now I don't even get a grin.
I see the way she wants you,
Like she did me way back when...

I see the way she looks,
When we go by your buddies shop.
I see the way she hurries off,
When I get to work at 7 o'clock.
I see the way she gets lost,
In those songs she listens too.
I know she'll always love me,
But I see the way she loves you….

I confronted her this evening,
Don't worry she finally told the truth.
It took a while to get through denial,
But she admitted that she loved you.
Just treat her good mister,
Show her that your love is real.
I can see the way she wants you,
So prove to her how you feel.

I see the way she hesitates,
Before saying "I love you" now.
I see the way her shortcuts,
Take the longer routes around.
I see the way she laughs and smiles,
The way she use to do.
I know she'll always love me,
But I see the way she loves you...

I know she'll always love me,
But I see the way she loves you…..

Through With You

Honey this morning when I woke up,
And started out that door.
I got this cold hearted chill,
Like I've never had before.
I caught the ice in your stare,
From across the room.
Then I heard you say "I don't care",
"If we are through."

Well open the door, Get out the glad locks;
Put some boxes in my truck…
You made the mistake, Of walking away;
Now I'm packing up…
Well open the door, Get out of the way;
So that I can get through…
I've had way too much, Of this childish stuff;
Honey I'm through with you…

Honey when I hug you now,
You just turn away.
You won't even kiss me,
Unless I turn my face.
I know you've found somebody,
Who's loving up on you.
So now even I don't care,
If we are through…

Well open the door,
Bag up some clothes;
Let's get this show on the road…
You made the mistake,
Of walking away;
So now I'm letting go…
Open the door,
Get out of the way;
I've got better things to do…
I've had way too much,
Of this childish stuff;
Honey I'm through with you…

Yeah honey I'm through with you….

Throw It At Me

Go ahead throw it at me,
Let me see what you have.
I'm not worried I'm committed,
To the family I won't let pass.
I'm not running around on you,
My love for you is real.
So go ahead throw it at me,
Let me know how you feel…

Do you love him are you sure,
You better make sure you're on solid ground.
I'm telling you now when I turn my back,
I'm not turning back around.
Don't threaten me with custody,
There my kids and they'll always be.
Let me know how you feel,
Go ahead throw it at me…

Go ahead throw it at me,
Let's hear all those nasty names.
I'm not worried about your allegations,
I'm not the one who's playing games.
I've always been faithful,
Because my love for you is real.
So go ahead throw it at me,
Let me know how you feel.

Do you love him are you sure,
You better make sure you're on solid ground.
I'm telling you now when I turn my back,
I'm not turning back around.
Don't threaten me with custody,
There my kids and they'll always be.
Let me know how you feel,
Go ahead throw it at me…

Yeah the vase the phone,
Whatever it may be.
Go ahead,
Throw it at me……

Nobody Plays The Part

I've lived my life for others,
For long enough.
I heard that in my head,
When I woke up.
I've given and I've helped,
Man it refreshes my heart.
But when I am down,
Nobody plays the part...
I've got a mother I've leaned on,
For too many years.
I've got two brothers who made it good,
Far away from here.
I've got one friend that I trust,
I've got one I love with all my heart.
But when I'm down,
Nobody plays the part....

Nobody plays the part,
So I play the fool.
That's how it seems to go,
My whole life through.
God I think you cursed me,
With this caring heart.
Cause when I'm in need,
Nobody plays the part.

I've got two little girls,
That's grown up and moved on.
I've got a son that's my pride and joy,
Man he has grown.
I've got a million children,
Who have a piece of my heart.
But when I'm down,
Nobody plays the part.

God I'm beaten and broken,
I wish I could go back to the start.
Cause when I'm down,
Nobody plays the part....

Closest Thing To Normal

Today I bow my head for a good friend,
One I've never met in my life.
A young lady who's struggled more than I,
Today those doctors are going to fix it right.
I woke with a prayer in my heart lord,
I had that precious face in my mind.
I could see her clapping her hands and being happy,
Singing along to these songs of mine.
I chatted with her mother a time or two,
I told her everything would be ok.
Now I'm begging you to watch over Kimberly,
Guide that doctors' hand today.

Lord this one is for Kimberly,
Let that young lady have some peace.
Her mother says she just wants to be normal,
Well Hun you're the closest thing to normal…I've ever seen.

Today I gathered around that cell phone,
Waiting on word that she was alright.
Logged on to Facebook and found her,
Smiling like a beacon in the night.
I hope that my songs bring you joy,
I hope that god brings you peace.
I hope that your mother out does us all,
And brings you a bowl of ice cream.
I'll be here waiting word of how you're doing,
I don't have no bigger plans in my way.
So lord please watch over Kimberly,
Guide those doctors' hands today.

Lord this one is for Kimberly,
Let that young lady have some peace.
Her mother says she just wants to be normal,
Well Hun you're the closest thing to normal….I've ever seen.

Don't worry what others call normal,
You're the closest thing to normal….I've ever seen….

Need You Today

(Chuck's Song)

It seems as though you've been gone for years,
my heart aches so much.
I still want to hear your voice,
and I long for your touch.
I know someday we'll be together,
but I don't know if I can wait.
I need your strength
and your love here today......
We shared so many memories;
the walls show me the times.
When I could look into those eyes of yours,
knowing everything would be fine.
I look at all the precious moments,
we shared in every way.
I need your strength
and your love here today....
(Chorus)
today when I wake up,
I will need you by my side.
Today when I rise up,
I will need you along for the ride.
Today is gonna be painful,
and make it....I just may.
But one thing's for certain,
I need you today....
The grass is getting taller,
I've never worried about that before.
There are trees that need to be trimmed,
before those spring time storms.
Yeah I've come to realize,
I miss you in so many ways.
One thing is so clear,
I need you today.....
Yeah one thing is for certain,
I still need you today....

Box Me Up

Good morning my little town of Lula,
not quite as big as those Nashville lights.
Still its home for the heart and soul,
it's where I've spent many wonderful nights.
I've walked these streets for going on 33 years;
I was 7 when we moved to this town.
Now it holds my dreams and a few tears,
every time that old train comes around.

So box me up and ship me home to Lula,
tell Nashville I enjoyed my time there.
I can write my songs from right there on the front porch,
sitting in my favorite rocking chair.
Tell all the folks down on Broadway,
that they lost a good soulful writer today.
Just box me up and ship me home to Lula,
my hometown Lula, GA.....
Tell my favorite neighbors that I love them,
their like a mom and dad to me.
Tell my mom that I think the world of her,
and I'm as happy as a man like me can be.
Just give me a pen and a notebook,
maybe a laptop will do.
Then I could still write from the heart,
bringing all of my songs home to you.

Just box me up and ship me home to Lula,
tell Nashville I enjoyed my time there.
I can write my songs from right there on the front porch,
sitting in my favorite rocking chair.
Tell all the folks down on Broadway,
that they lost a good soulful writer today.
Just box me up and ship me home to Lula,
my hometown Lula, GA......
Lay me to rest under that old pine tree,
let my headstone say.
Here lies a man enjoying his surroundings,
in his hometown of Lula, GA......

Cindy's Cove

Sitting down near the water,
a cold drink in hand.
Watching the kids playing,
in gods beautiful land.
This place it holds magic,
like many never know.
Tucked back in the woods of the mountains,
a little place called Cindy's cove......

Where God talks to your heart,
with the chirping of the birds...
might even see a deer or three,
if we don't speak no words.
Got a cool river stream running,
I often wonder where it goes.
Running through the Georgia mountains,
To a place called Cindy's cove.....

Got a little radio playing,
cranking out those country hits.
Got a line out in the water,
but I ain't getting any hits.
God to me this is heaven,
I just wanted you to know.
My own little piece of paradise,
right here at Cindy's cove...

Where God talks to your heart,
with the chirping of the birds...
might even see a deer or three,
if we don't speak no words.
Got a cool river stream running,
I often wonder where it goes.
Running through the Georgia Mountains,
To a place called Cindy's cove.....

So pull out the old tent,
grab a sleeping bag and we'll go.
To paradise on earth,
little place called Cindy's cove......

Thanks for the inspiration to Donnie Rogers
The best neighbor in the world

Another Day Of Hell

It was another day in the office,
another mile on the road.
Another innocent soul dying,
another politician lie told.
It was another chance at freedom,
another insane cell.
Yeah today, was just another day of hell......

It was another 12 hour shift,
another 60 hour week.
Another chance to stand up…
another chance to speak…
It was another wrong direction,
another story to tell.
Yeah today, was another day of hell...

Another day in the glowing flames,
Praying God would come and save me.
Another chance to take his hand,
And pray he would take me.
It was another time left wondering,
If I was talking to myself.
Yeah today, was another day of hell...

It was another friend I couldn't help,
Another mouth I couldn't feed.
Another chance for me to give…
Another family in need…
It was a long drawn out process,
Another test I'm sure to fail.
Yeah today, was another day of hell...

Another day in the glowing flames,
Praying God would come and save me.
Another chance to take his hand,
And pray he would take me.
It was another time left wondering,
If I was talking to myself.
Yeah today, was another day of hell...

Lord I hope you hear me praying,
I can't do this by myself.
And today, was another day of hell…
Yeah today, was just another day of hell…

My Time

A loving heart and caring soul,
A mind that just ran free.
An awesome dad who revolved his world,
Around those 3.
A poetic heart by nature,
Genius at writing his rhymes.
Yeah that's how I want to be remembered;
When it's my time...

A man that loved his children,
And made sure they knew he cared.
A man that gave all he could,
And shared all he could share.
A man who loved one woman,
'Til he got left behind.
Yeah that's how I want to be remembered,
When it's my time....

When it's my time to go,
Don't cry a single tear.
'Cause I'll be free at home,
Far away from here.
I'll be playing guitar,
And starring up in the sky.
Don't cry for me,
When it's my time

A man that got along,
And never liked to fight.
A man who was home,
With his family every night.
A man that would give his last breath,
To protect them from any crime.
Yeah that's how I want to be remembered,
When it's my time...

When it's my time to go,
Don't cry a single tear.
'Cause I'll be free at home,
Far away from here.
I'll be playing guitar,
And starring up in the sky.
Don't cry for me,
When it's my time.

Yeah I'll be playing guitar, And singing at the top of my lungs.
Don't cry for me, When my time comes......

Keep Dixie Flying

First they banned St. Andrew's Cross......
They called it Stars and Bars.
Now they've forgotten all those lost.....
They claim heritage would be hard.
Now I'm not out to start trouble.....
But there's some folks out here lying.
There's nothing racist left in the rubble.....
So let's keep Dixie Flying!!!!

Fly it from rooftops,
And the flagpole where it belongs.
Fly it for your ancestor,
Who proudly passed it on.
Fly it with pride my son,
For those who died fighting.
As life comes and passes on,
Let's keep Dixie Flying!!!!

No now I'm not no racist.....
And I'm a GOD fearing man.
I don't belong to no social club......
Just to...GOD's Klan.
I'm sure you have your opinion.....
But I also have mine.
This is one old boy who sees nothing wrong.....
With keeping Dixie Flying!!!!

Fly it from rooftops,
And the flagpole where it belongs.
Fly it for your ancestor,
Who proudly passed it on.
Fly it with pride my son,
For those who died fighting.
As life comes and passes on,
Let's keep Dixie Flying!!!!

For all the heroes who died fighting,
Let's keep Dixie Flying!!!!!!!

Across The Street

It's that time of year, the solicitations have begun.
Let's help the homeless, before winter comes.
Now I'm not rich, I'm nobody with fame.
Half of my own family...doesn't remember my name.
Still here I am, right across the street.
From some charity Santa, looking down at me.
Day in day out, I watch the crowd go by.
To shun old Saint Nick, for a shiny new dime.
I hear all the rumors, the wishes...the lies.
The homeless needs your donation, before winter arrives.
I hear the wisecracks, like go get a job.
I work for my money; I deserve what I've got.
So I count down the months, 'til Christmas arrives.
I start my list, at the end of July.
I save all the pennies, nickels, and dimes.
To do my little share, to do something nice.
Every year I wait, for December to come.
To kick my plan in gear, before Christmas is gone.
Then on a winter evening, just before nightfall.
I put my donation, into the kettle at the Mall.
Along with the money, I leave a little note.
That says Dear Santa, this will help I hope.
Signed with Faith and Love, to one and to all.
From the homeless man in the box,
Across the street from the Mall!!!
~The End~

*Dedicated to all those who strive to make a difference in someone else's life regardless of financial status. In memory of a good person and my friend Ms. Sandra Stephens.
~Your Memory WILL Live on!

If That Describes Hell

I hear you yelling, but the ballgames still on.
Are the kids bathed, is my dinner done?
What's that? Go where? Well honey don't threaten me!
Trust me if I wake in the morning,
That's exactly where I'll be………

Where the flames….burn hotter every day.
And there's pain….and suffering along the way.
Where everyone you love, acts like they no longer care.
If that describes hell…..I'm there!!!!!

Yes, I know, this evening you've made plans.
And you'll be home late, once again.
I'm sure that Wal-Mart, is running low.
After all that's supposedly,
Where you go.

What's that? Not again….I told you how that goes.
I don't need directions….That's a very familiar road.
Filled with potholes….of lost hope.
If that describes hell….Welcome home!!

If you think it's hell….You're not alone!!!

Man Like No Other

He starts his night, already in a fight;
With a machine….that's not even turned on.
Makes his co-worker friends, all just with;
That for once….he would just stay home!!

He's an alright guy, seems most of the time;
But a genius….he certainly is not.
He fights through the pain, of the daily strain;
That he believes….only he has got!!

He's a man like no other….It just makes me wonder;
How he keeps from going off??
Still don't know what's wrong….his machine still ain't on;
Still he swears it's not his fault.
I hate to blow his cover…
But he's a man… like no other!!!

5:00 o'clock rolls round, one more hour to shoot down;
Before I'm home….under my cover.
I just can't wait, to simply get away;
From a man….like no other!!!

He's a man like no other….It just makes me wonder;
How he keeps from going off??
Still don't know what's wrong….his machine still ain't on;
Still he swears it's not his fault.
I hate to blow his cover…
But he's a man… like no other!!!

I feel sorry, for his dear sweet mother;
For giving birth….like no other!!!

Writer's Block

I was listening to the radio, sitting there at my home.
When all of a sudden...the music stopped...
The power had gone out, the kids started to shout.
Then my concentration...was lost....

Started up once again, a hit tune in my head.
And words started flowing...from my ink pen...
Down to my last line, I'll finish up in time.
To see the race going...on ESPN...

I'M a writing...Music loving guy.
I'm a fighting...With every single line.
It's never been this hard, Shout...it's twelve o'clock...
I'll finish it up tomorrow...I've got writer's block!!!!!!

The sunrise hits me, wakes me from my sleep.
I rush to my notebook...wearing only my socks...
Start to write that last line, when the idea slips my mind.
Just my luck...I've got writer's block!!!

I'M a writing...Music loving guy.
I'm a fighting...With every single line.
It's never been this hard, Shout...it's twelve o'clock...
I'll finish it up tomorrow...I've got writer's block!!!!!!

I'll finish it tomorrow,
Today...I've go writer's block!!!

His Better Half

He hugs his son, says "I've got to go."
Then it's out the door, and down the road.
He hates to leave, but those bills won't pay themselves....
Comes dragging in, sends them on their way.
Try getting some sleep, while they're away.
After cleaning up and dusting off the shelves....
He knows inside.....he would really enjoy some help!!!!

Their mother...well...she'll be waiting.
He's not looking to replace her love.
Just someone ...he can talk too.
When times start getting rough.
He tries his best to hide it....
But his children all see his pain.
He's half the man he used to be...
Since his better half went away...

He talks to her picture, he laughs and he cries.
Remembering all those memories, of good and bad time.
Sometimes it's like; she's sitting there by his side...
Indulges the children, when they find him a date.
They think he's unhappy, but really he ain't.
'Cause he know that soon...he'll be back with his bride...

'Cause their mother will be waiting...
He's not looking to replace her love.
Just someone he can talk too,
When times start getting rough.
He tries his best to hide it,
But his children all see his pain.
He's half the man he used to be,
Since his better half went away.....

Yeah he's half the man he used to be...
Since his better half went away.........

Baby Doll

She was a sweet child to her mother, a true blessing from above.
A gift from the heavens, a true bundle of love.
She was the strength her mama needed, while going through rough times.
And because of her she was happy, when she spread her wings to fly.......

They call her Mikayla...
I call her Baby Doll...
She's now 11 years old...man she's getting tall!
She's an artist like her mother....she helps make sense of it all.
They call her Mikayla....
I call her baby doll.

The oldest of all my young ones, I know I'm tough on her.
I understand when she's angry, but I'm tough because I love her.
Someday my little angel...will spread her wings and fly.
Then I'll stand there a proud father, with a tear welling in my eye.

They may call her Mikayla...
I still call her Baby Doll...
Going off to start her own life...I hope she remembers to call.
An artist for the gallery now...I guess she's no longer small.
They call her Mikayla...
I call her Baby Doll...

Yes, they call her Mikayla...
I still call her Baby Doll...

*Dedicated to my oldest daughter Mikayla Dawn Sargent.
I am proud of you and I love you with all of my heart.*
~Love Daddy~

Lottery Winner

I took my time, waiting in line;
'Til the opportunity comes along…..
Filled out my card, with my numbers and a heart;
Before I passed it on….
I watched your eyes, light up with surprise;
You said yes to a movie and dinner….
What do you know my friend, my numbers finally came in;
I'm a Lottery Winner!!!!!

I won those numbers, I won her heart;
I won me a friend for life…..
I won myself, a brand new start;
When I won you for my wife…..
I'll never forget, how nervous I was;
As for as dating I was a beginner……
But it sure paid off, I thank God;
For making me a Lottery Winner.

Years have passed, my friends all ask;
Doesn't those same numbers get old…..
I just smile with pride, 'case deep down inside;
Those numbers saved this soul……

I won those numbers, I won her heart;
I won me a friend for life…..
I won myself, a brand new start;
When I won you for my wife…..
I'll never forget, how nervous I was;
As for as dating I was a beginner……
But it sure paid off, I thank God;
For making me a Lottery Winner.

Yeah, it sure paid off,
I'm a Lottery Winner!!!!!

Arching For Miranda

I saw you on the TV….singing your 1st song.
My heart went and skipped a beat….
Heard a reporter ask "Are you single?"…If so it won't be long.
'Til the young men are bowing at your feet….
I remember the thought that was running through my mind;
"Boy you've got to find that girl……"
So I've added up the cost, to leave Lula Georgia Behind;
-And tomorrow I'll explore a new world….

I'm on a search for Miranda….
I saw her on CMT…
My eyes 'bout popped out of my head…
And my heart skipped a beat…

Before I knew it, she was high on the charts;
Looking pretty singing "kerosene"…
Maybe I'll write a hit, that strikes a chord in her heart;
Then maybe she'll be on a search for me…

As for now I'm searching for Miranda…
I saw her on GAC….
My eyes 'bout popped out of my head…
And my heart skipped a beat…

Yes, I'm on a search for Miranda…who knows…
Maybe she's searching for me!!!!

10,000 Miles From Home

Dear Mother…..this here's your baby boy;
I'm writing to tell you I'm fine…
How's my brother…. is dad still annoyed;
That I didn't listen this time….
Most days I'll admit….it's a living hell;
Something I hope you'll never know…
I hope you'll write a bit….oh well….I guess I've got to go…

Back to being all by myself…
Tucked away in my own fox hole.
Keep us all in your prayers…
We could use the help.
After all…we're 10, 000 miles from home!!!!

I remember dad….telling us all stories;
About the bad things from Vietnam…
I've seen the bad; I've seen the gory;
But don't worry I'm not harmed…
Dad's right…this isn't like his war;
There's oil fields laid out in rows…
The fight….they've called it desert storm;
Write soon…..I've got to go…..

Back to being all by myself…
Tucked away in my own fox hole.
Keep us all in your prayers…
We could use the help.
After all…we're 10, 000 miles from home!!!!
We could use your prayers….10,000 miles from home!!!

Dedicated to the brave men and women of The United States Military.
From past to present, you are all heroes and I for one pray you have heard every one…
10,000 miles from home.

Knowing You

Knowing you…made this country stronger.
You brought respect…from leaders around the globe!
Knowing you…made us believe a little longer;
That we were safe…from all the dangers we know!

Knowing you…we believed your message.
You kept your work…like so few politicians do!
Knowing you…taught us a valuable lesson;
That in this land…dreams do come true.

So now we say thanks…Mr. President.
May you rest in peace…while we as a nation salute!
I pray you now…that for us you were Heaven sent;
And we are a better nation…for knowing you!

~The End~

6-11-06
In memory of our 40th President… Mr. Ronald Reagan…1911-2004.
~~~RIP…Mr. President~~~

The Junk Jockey

He hauls the cars up the highway… straight out of Lula, GA.
His friends all call him "Jimmy"…He wouldn't have it any other way.
Sits around at the local store…just shooting all the bull.
Nicknamed "The Junk Jockey"…for the cars that he pulls.

He's a hometown legend….with a lore;
Like none that he's ever caught me…
Sells the cars…like nobody before;
He is "The" Junk Jockey…..

Respects the town…respects the people…respects the life we all enjoy.
One stop light and two church steeples….Perfect for one hometown boy.
Says he's hauled 'em all…Toyotas, Chevys, and Fords.
That's how he got the name…A Junk Jockey like none before.

He's a hometown legend….with a lore;
Like none that he's ever caught me…
Sells the cars…like nobody before;
He is "The" Junk Jockey…..

If you need a car….he's your man;
But he's Lula's own Junk Jockey!!!!

~Written by Mitchell B. Cooper ~
~Titled by Mr." Jimmy" Bruce

The Meanest Woman I Know

She called me a slacker…I threw the keys at her;
And told her there's the door…
I didn't won't to kiss her…I didn't think I' miss her,
Now I'm lonelier than ever before…
I tried going dating…she was right there waiting;
Out on that hardwood floor…
I think I felt her slap me…I think I heard her laughing;
Why am I on the floor?

My baby just slapped me…punched me in the eye;
I think she even spit on me too….
She said she just tapped me…we'll officer that's a lie;
Look here my eyes are black and blue…
I don't want to press charges…that's a little too harsh;
I'm a man I can handle my own…
I don't mean to barge…could you walk me to my car;
'Cause she's the meanest woman I know…

Said she got angry…'cause I was being lazy;
That's what started this fight…
Said for me not to pout…about her going out;
She was staying at a friend's tonight…
I figured I'd meet some friends…before my one night ends;
Maybe have 'em over for the game…
Look at me now…outside my own house;
Hey baby why's the locks been changed…

My baby just slapped me…punched me in the eye;
I think she even spit on me too….
She said she just tapped me…we'll officer that's a lie;
Look here my eyes are black and blue…
I don't want to press charges…that's a little too harsh;
I'm a man I can handle my own…
I don't mean to barge…could you walk me to my car;
'Cause she's the meanest woman I know…

If you don't mind…could you keep her a night?
'Cause she's the Meanest Woman I know!!!!

I've Been Blessed

I've worked real hard…nearly all of my life;
Building cabinets and sacking feed….
But sitting alone in the yard…thinking up songs to write;
That's where life best suits me…

I've made me a million…at 31 years old;
Who am I to complain…?
I've got 3 beautiful children…two places I call home;
And an angel guiding the way…..

I've been blessed….I've been thankful;
I've tried to be kind to others…
I've been tested…by the unfaithful;
But I've remained a low key undercover…
I may have to miss my best friend…but I'm convinced;
That's just part of the test…
Yeah, if my life ends…don't cry friend;
I've been blessed…

Now the road I'm on…I hope it takes me;
Somewhere far from the pain…
I only hope…that what awaits me;
Leaves me feeling blessed again…

I've been blessed….I've been thankful;
I've tried to be kind to others…
I've been tested…by the unfaithful;
But I've remained a low key undercover…
I may have to miss my best friend…but I'm convinced;
That's just part of the test…
Yeah, if my life ends…don't cry friend;
I've been blessed…

If my life ends…don't cry for me friend;
Rest assured I've been blessed….

Unscrewed

I broke it all down…it about broke me.
The tiny thing inside…that we call belief.
I believed in my talents…I believed in gaining wealth.
Now it's at hand…and I can't help myself………

Honey! What am I gonna do…….
Can you get me unscrewed……?

Can you unscrew those troubles…I nailed in so deep?
Can you unscrew those memories…that won't let me sleep.
I know I ask a lot…but this time I'm begging you.
Can you help me out, honey…can you get me unscrewed…..

I fought back the tears…they fought back with pain.
I swear that my own ears…heard my heart break.
I watched all of my passion…just melting away.
I listened to my mouth…not knowing what to say.

I'm asking what am I gonna do……
Can you get me unscrewed……..

Can you unscrew those troubles…I nailed in so deep?
Can you unscrew those memories…that won't let me sleep.
I know I ask a lot…but this time I'm begging you.
Can you help me out, honey…can you get me unscrewed…..

Yes I'm begging you…can you get me unscrewed……..

Stranger From A Friends

The weekend is over…no more time with the kids.
Come tomorrow evening…the workweek begins.
Same old routine…that I've done so many years…..

Rise and shine…with breakfast in the air.
The scent of brown gravy…makes its way up stairs.
Where it finds me in dreams…thankful that you're here….

I may not be perfect…or give a lot of my time.
But I work really hard…for this family of mine.
Four girls, one boy…and a stranger from a friends……

I'm not asking to be married…that may come with time.
But I know when I get home…it's you I hope to find.
From the present day…'til my life ends……..

No, I may not be perfect…I may never find time.
But I'll always work hard…to feed this family of mine.
Four girls, one boy…and a stranger from a friends….
We'll see how it goes…from now 'til my life ends….

We'll see how it goes…with my stranger from a friends!!!!

I Ain't Going Nowhere

I called you up…early this morning;
Said baby doll…I think we need to talk……
I don't like…the way we've been going;
My heart thinks it's time…to take a walk….

No now….you ain't did nothing;
It's just…deep down it don't feel right….
I've thought about it…I finally thought of something;
Maybe you and I…can talk tonight……

I ain't going nowhere without you…
I've done committed all of my heart.
But the attitudes don't help make it better…
I ain't going nowhere unless you start!!!

You see girl…for years I've been alone;
Never dreamed…I would meet someone again……
Then there you were….at a friend's home;
Banging and screaming let me in……

Sometimes…I may lose my cool girl;
But I cool off…real quick when I walk….
In my eyes…I'm a good guy in this world;
So tonight…maybe you and I can talk…….

I ain't going nowhere without you…
I've done committed all of my heart.
But the attitudes don't help make it better…
I ain't going nowhere unless you start!!!

No I ain't going nowhere….unless you start!!!!

I Come To Life

Alone with my thoughts…a notebook and pen….
My true definition…of the word Heaven…
I can speak to a heart…without saying a work…
GOD did his part…by granting me the gift that's unheard…

I come to life in poetry….
I live through my songs…
I come to life in poetry…
There's no way such a gift can be wrong!!!!!

I've written thousands of poems…hundreds of songs.
One Alma Mater…for a school back home.
I've written Plaques for government…for DUI schools.
Words from the heart…that can make other hearts move……..

And I come to life in poetry….
I live through my songs…
Yes, I come to life in poetry…
There's no way such a gift could be wrong!!!

I reckon I'll be writing….'til I'm gone!!!

The Exchange

Sitting here in my pickup…got my best bud by my side.
The one blessing I have…from that deviled ex-bride.
Got the neon sign flashing…blinking out that Texaco name.
It's the same 'ole story just a different week…down at the exchange….

The place you go cash your check…that I work so hard for.
No reason we meet here…that's why it's your favorite store.
Just looking at the other dads…in their trucks doing the same.
It's just that time of the week…down at the exchange!!!

Strap him in your backseat…then give him a little peck.
Then proceed on over to your side…to give you another check.
Step on back and wave goodbye…as I watch you roll away.
Same routine every time…down at the exchange……..

The place you go cash that check…that I work so hard for.
No reason that we meet here…that's why it's your favorite store.
Just looking at the other dads…in the parking lot doing the same.
It's just that time of the week…down at the exchange!!!!!!

Yeah, it's that time of the week….
Down at the exchange……..

Inspired by Richard Hanes

That's How Life Goes... In A Country Sort Of Way

Taking life in stride, like it's supposed to go.
Not a roller coaster ride, just a simple stroll.
Breathe that clean mountain air, while the children run and play.
That's how life goes, in a country sort of way.....

Work those twelve hour shifts, down at the mill.
Then scrape up those pennies, just to pay the bills.
It's a laid back life, free from the problems of today.
That's how life goes, in a country sort of way.....

It's yes sir, yes mam'....to your mom and dad.
It's blood and sweat...to provide for the family you have.
It's church on Sundays...to confess your sins away.
That's how life goes...in a country sort of way!!!

Now the moments closer, today is the day.
We'll walk that aisle together, and I'll give you away.
With a warning and a handshake, to tell him something I'm sure he knows.
In a country sort of way, that's how life goes.....

It's yes sir, yes mam'....to your mom and dad.
It's blood and sweat...to provide for the family you have.
It's church on Sundays...to confess your sins away.
That's how life goes...in a country sort of way!!!

That's how life goes....
In a country sort of way!!!!!!

Being In Love

Used to be….I could work all night;
Never losing sight of the task…..
Now it's plain to see…I'm not alright;
But I'll say different if asked….

It's a hell of a load…that's on my shoulders;
Still I can't get enough…..
I guess that's how it goes…that's why I've told her;
That I'm enjoying being in love…….

Being in love is a blessing, especially when you're loved back.
It's the one thing that can save a man, and get him back on track.
No there's nothing else like it, it's truthfully a gift from above.
There's no use trying to fight it, the feeling of being in love…..

For years…a man would be so tough;
Making the women chase him….
'Til the tears…started welling up'
From the pain he's holding in…..

I don't know…but I think I've found it;
My angel from above….
I only hope…I can stand my ground;
'Cause I like being in love……

Being in love is a blessing, especially when you're loved back.
It's the one thing that can save a man, and get him back on track.
No there's nothing else like it, it's truthfully a gift from above.
There's no use trying to fight it, the feeling of being in love…..

There's no use trying to fight it,
The feeling of being in love……..

With My Guitar

Sitting down at the park, with no children around.
A perfect time for the heart, to jot some things down.
Honey, I feel so lonely, since you walked away.
But it's nearly 5 o'clock Friday, so wherever you've gone please stay......

'Cause I'm gonna cry all night, at some strangers bad jokes.
And come morning light, I want you to know.
I'll be fine by myself....with my guitar!!!!.
Tonight I'm gonna cry some tears, due to all the smoke.
I'm gonna wish you were here, to hear every word and note.
But tomorrow I'll be fine....with my guitar!!!!!

5 o'clock it's time to party, so I head on home.
Clear my mind and scrub my body, put my old boots on.
Tell your picture I hope you're happy, don't come back girl it's too late.
It's 5 o'clock Friday, so please just stay.......

'Cause I'm gonna cry all night, at some strangers bad jokes.
And come morning light, I want you to know.
I'll be fine by myself....with my guitar!!!!.
Tonight I'm gonna cry some tears, due to all the smoke.
I'm gonna wish you were here, to hear every word and note.
But tomorrow I'll be fine....with my guitar!!!!!

Yeah, tomorrow I'll be fine...with my guitar!!!!!

Woman I Could Love You

Alone on my trusty old barstool, talking it up and having a time.
I told the boss what I think about you, you're artwork in my mind.
The way you seem so friendly, makes my heart flutter each day.
I can't express the feelings within me, but I'll try my best to say.

Woman, I could love you……Woman, I need you.
My whole life would be OK….If I could just see you.
Woman, I could hold you…Like you would want a good man to do.
Woman, I could love you…could you love me too……..

Friday nights just around the corner, I'm working up my nerves to ask.
Would you like to go out to dinner, Or maybe somewhere to dance.
You had my heart at my first glance; I would hate to watch you slip away.
I'm not real good at expressing myself, but I'll try my best to say…….

Woman, I could love you…Woman, I need you.
My whole life would be OK…If I could just see you.
Woman, I could hold you…Like you would want a good man to do.
Woman, I could love you…Could you love me too…..

Woman, I could love you…Could you love me too!

Summertime

Another week gone by, the weekend is here.
Time to unwind, and have an ice cold beer.
Load up the boat, the cooler...the grill.
We're gonna have us, a summertime thrill.

Call up the children, say come on let's go.
Bring your good friends, to the swimming hole.
Kick back and relax, in my good 'ole lawn chair.
We're gonna have a ball, summertime is here!!!!

There for the beaches, the bikinis, the girls.
Time for those steamy nights,
Out of this world
It's time to have fun,
Free from worries or cares.
C'mon and getcha some!!!
The summertime is here!!!.

Crank up some tunes, some Chesney or Strait.
Fire up some dogs, on the grill by the lake.
Kick back, relax, let yourself unwind.
Let's have a toast, to the summertime!!!!

There for the beaches, the bikinis, the girls.
Time for those steamy nights,
Out of this world
It's time to have fun,
Free from worries or cares.
C'mon and getcha some....
The summertime is here.

C'mon and getcha some!!!
Summertime is here!!!!

By Her Side

Sometimes I stop to wonder, about things out of my control.
Like world peace, calm in the Middle East;
Things that I'll never know....
I know that I ask a lot of you, and I patiently wait for a reply.
So now I must ask you, a question or two;
So that I can get on with life....

Do you let her hear me talking, can she watch the children grow.
Is she certain my loves not stopping, just because my heart is broke.
Does she still sing like an angel, can she bring tears to your eyes.
Lord, please steer her from danger, 'til I'm back home by her side...

I still talk to those pictures; I still expect that phone to ring.
Then hearing her voice, giving me a choice;
Of exactly what I want to eat......
I still smell her perfume, in the bedroom on her clothes.
So now I must ask you, a question or two;
So that I can move on......

Do you let her hear me talking, can she watch the children grow.
Is she certain my loves not stopping, just because my heart is broke.
Does she still sing like an angel, can she bring tears to your eyes.
Lord, please steer her from danger, 'til I'm back home by her side...

Please steer her from danger,
'Til I'm back home by her side......

Hope you found a few stories
That made you laugh, Cry, Sing,
Or just think....Oh yeah that's me.

And I hope to have more for you soon.
Thanks for being my first readers.

Mitchell B. Cooper, writer of poetry & song

The End

Printed in the United States
By Bookmasters